The Gift of New Creation
LENT

The Gift of New Creation

THOMAS L. EHRICH

A Lenten Study Based on the Revised Common Lectionary

Abingdon Press / Nashville

THE GIFT OF NEW CREATION
BY THOMAS L. EHRICH

A Lenten Study Based on the Revised Common Lectionary

Copyright © 2018 by Abingdon Press

ISBN-13: 9781501870903

18 19 20 21 22 23 24 25 26 27—10 9 8 7 6 5 4 3 2 1

MANUFACTURED IN THE UNITED STATES OF AMERICA

Contents

Introduction

Every book has a context. From the books of Scripture to the rules of cards, a book rises from the dust and muck, glory and hope of a moment in time and a writer living that moment.

You deserve to know the context for this book. I wrote it on the road, during a 4,100-mile cross-country pilgrimage in search of fresh ideas, fresh words, and fresh faith. I call it "Fresh Day on the Road." My separate book on the trek is called *Two-Lane Theology*.

For a month, beginning in San Francisco and pointing east toward New York, I started each day deciding where to go next on the two-lane roads of America. Along the way each day, I stopped to look around. Or I chose not to stop, depending on what I found. I ate here and there, engaged people in conversation, or just drove in the silence of my thoughts.

Each evening, I stopped at a hotel, usually in a small town, with Internet access and a tasty diner nearby. There I wrote the reflections and Bible studies that comprise this book.

I had no idea at the outset what that would mean. Would the Bible sound different in New Mexico? Would the sight of people going about their lives in Oklahoma shape what I heard in Scripture? Would my authorial ideas for your growth change when I crossed the Mississippi River or the Mason-Dixon Line?

I planned to write each day, making the day's miles the context. My hope is that you will read this book in the same way: coming to it each day with whatever your day's journey has given you. If it has been a great day, read the lessons with the confidence and optimism that a great day can instill. Or read with the confusion and anxiety that a bad day can instill. Let your encounter with God's Word be a living journey, fresh each day.

I wrote with your faith and personal transformation in mind. I don't believe our call is to become experts in the Bible or in its exegesis. Our call, I believe, is to draw closer to God, and to allow God to transform our lives more and more into God's likeness, God's love, and God's way of being. The Bible opens doors to that transformation. The Bible gives us glimpses of what that transformation looks like. Biblical experts do exist, and I think we can learn from them. But first things first. Faith comes from submission to God, not from expertise in biblical studies. I hope to raise questions that intrigue you intellectually and to offer real-world glimpses of God that engage you emotionally, which point you toward a spiritual connection with God.

We will be using the lessons laid out by the Revised Common Lectionary for Lent and Easter Day. In the three-year cycle, these are the readings from year C. We will consider three lessons each week. The first will come from the Old Testament; many weeks it will be from the Book of the prophet Isaiah. The second will come from various writings attributed to Paul, the New Testament Epistles. And the third will come from the Gospels, primarily from the Gospel of Luke.

Each week's lessons have a unifying theme. Preachers who use the lectionary often try to identify that theme and use it as the ground of their preaching. The act of preaching is an analogy to what we are undertaking in writing and reading this book. For the preacher has a context: the world beyond church doors, the life of the faith community, and his or her own life. The best preaching tries to engage all of these elements: Scripture, culture, life in the marketplace, the faith community's joys and sorrows and questions, and what the preacher brings to the pulpit. The preacher's overarching aim is to draw people closer to God and to encourage the transformation of life that is God's great desire for them. That is my aim in writing this study: to help you draw closer to God and to encourage you to be transformed into God's likeness.

Like a pilgrimage with no set itinerary, engagement with the Bible can be disconcerting, sobering, uplifting, humbling, and more than a little dangerous. Delusions like control and certainty pass away. Easy answers fail to persuade. The small fragment of God that you have been content to grasp suddenly seems too little. You want more, but the more you want, the less you know; and the less you know for sure, the deeper you are willing to look. In the end, you can't just turn it off, put down the book, and go home again.

So beware. I literally have no advance itinerary for this driving pilgrimage and no advance agenda for this book. It is all about discovery. We will discover together, and we will find what we find.

Messy Faith

*Scriptures for the
First Sunday of Lent*
**Deuteronomy 26:1-11
Romans 10:8b-13
Luke 4:1-13**

The basic proposition of faith can be stated simply: God is in life, and we know God through life as we live it. We don't worship a God who is impossibly far from us, a God outside the human realm. We worship a God who is among us, a God known as *Emmanuel*, "God with us."

How did the ancient Hebrews know "I am" was their God? Because "I am" saw their suffering in Egypt, liberated them from bondage, brought them in safety to a Promised Land, and gave that land to them for their use. The fruits of that usage—crops from the land—bear witness to God's faithfulness.

How close is our God? "In your mouth and in your heart," said Paul. You have but to confess to God and call upon God's name, and God will bless you with faith.

How could Jesus understand and verify God's call to him? He went into the wilderness, did battle with the devil, and remembered what God had told him. Jesus just needed to live as God had told him to live.

Faith can get messy when it is this close to real life. It's easier to form beliefs from a great distance, where order can be imagined and doctrines inferred. It is much more difficult to seek God in the chaos and corruption of the here and now.

This week's lessons spring from gritty locales and tell stories of God in life. God is known in the offspring of a "starving Aramean" (Jacob). God is known in a word so near to us that it changes our lips and hearts. And God is known in a high-stakes contest between a newly baptized young Galilean and the forces of darkness itself.

A GRATEFUL PEOPLE
DEUTERONOMY 26:1-11

The challenge for any believer is to know what they believe and why they believe it. What happened that caused belief to master nonbelief? What changed that made a story grounded in faith seem more vital than a story grounded in, say, one's career or national pride?

Christians created creeds for this purpose. The Apostles' Creed and the Nicene Creed are the most widely used. They recount the nature of God and tell the narrative of Jesus, and in so doing they relate the impact God has on humankind.

The ancient Hebrews had a different kind of creed. We read it in the twenty-sixth chapter of Deuteronomy, a book presented as the farewell words of Moses as the Hebrews ended their wilderness wandering and prepared to enter the Promised Land of Canaan. Some have called these verses, Deuteronomy 26:5b-9, the "Deuteronomic Creed."

Moses envisioned a harvest festival after the Israelites' first growing season in the land of Canaan, a festival that would be repeated annually. The people were to gather their harvest, and then bring a portion of it to their holy place. They were to present the first portion (usually seen as the first tenth portion) to the priest. And then they were to explain why they took this action.

Their explanation took the form of telling their story as a people (Deuteronomy 26:5b-9). They were children of a "starving Aramean," namely, Jacob. As told in the Book of Genesis, in Israel's prehistory, the sons of Jacob went down to Egypt during a famine. Under Joseph's care they survived, and they eventually became a "great nation, mighty and numerous." But then a new Pharaoh appeared, and he turned the Hebrews into slaves and subjected them to "hard labor."

The people cried out to their God, and God heard them, saw their affliction, toil, and oppression, and decided to act. As told in the Book of Exodus, God performed great "signs and wonders," convincing Pharaoh to let God's people go. When Pharaoh changed his mind, God, "with a strong hand and an outstretched arm," parted the Reed Sea and led the Hebrews to safety. God brought them across the Sinai Desert to the River Jordan—a long journey that formed them as a people—and gave them the land of Canaan, "a land full of milk and honey."

THE GIFT OF NEW CREATION

So now they brought their offering to God in gratitude, both for the harvest and for the great acts of liberation and guidance that made it possible (Deuteronomy 26:10).

This creed explains what the people needed to know as Israelites. They were a people whose cries God heard. God had set them free from bondage. They would find themselves in bondage again, during their years in exile in Babylon. God would liberate them again and give them a land for planting. Note that God didn't promise them a powerful kingdom, but a land where they could provide for their needs.

They were a people whose duty was to use the land and to show gratitude for it. The heart of this creed is gratitude. It is not the might and majesty of Israel's God, nor is it some call to rule the world in God's name. The heart of the creed is Israel's duty to give back to God in thanksgiving.

Imagine how world history would have been different—and would be different now—if God's people understood themselves first and foremost as those who have been liberated and called to gratitude.

Instead of parading our excellence and right opinions, we would tell the story of our humiliation and God's response. Instead of presuming the right to rule others, we would plant our land and share the harvest with God. Instead of building bigger barns and grander castles, we would lay the first portion of our harvest before God.

Israel's ancient creed answers perhaps the greatest dilemma in which people find themselves: amnesia. We forget who we are. We forget our descent from the God of creation. We forget the deep love God has for all people. We forget that all we have comes from God. We forget our fundamental obligation to show gratitude for what we have received. We forget to be people of freedom in a world prone to bondage. We forget to go where God leads, rather than where appetite or bullies insist. We forget to do the work God has given us to do, and then be grateful for it and celebrate.

Instead, we allow others to define us—and to believe them when they sell us short. Instead, we take the credit for the good we have and blame God for the bad. We applaud ourselves. We accept bondage as the price we pay for getting the comfort and wealth we crave. We deny any need for gratitude, saying, "I did this, I alone." And we certainly don't intend to share our harvest. Rather than celebrate our good fortune, we lament all that we don't have.

It is appealing to define God by creeds of right opinion. It puts us in charge. Telling a story of liberation, on the other hand, a story of journey, harvest, and gratitude, has an entirely different impact. It acknowledges that we are not in charge. You can see why Moses laid two requirements before his people: Have a harvest festival, and give to God in gratitude. Imagine the family of an office worker or factory worker, or teacher or nurse, gathering each week to celebrate the week's paycheck, laying a portion of it before God and celebrating. Wouldn't that change family dynamics!

I personally resonate with this narrative creed in Deuteronomy more than the more definitional creeds of the Christian era. They describe the same God. The Hebrew creed focuses on God's faithfulness, as evident in acts of compassion, power, and steadfast love. The Christian creeds lend themselves to statements of doctrine. Unfortunately, people in our age—and perhaps every age—are susceptible to the malady that usually follows from doctrine, namely, right-opinion. We are all too easily convinced in reciting the creeds that we find favor with God by correctly defining God's characteristics and knowing how the Trinitarian parts fit together.

The Deuteronomic Creed, on the other hand, points to God and tells a story of divine providence at work. That speaks to the bondage I experience. It is different from the Hebrews' bondage in Egypt, but because this is a narrative, I can make the intuitive leap to my own form of bondage. I can place myself in the creed.

Faith, then, becomes the act of recognizing the moment of liberation at hand and following God's mediator across the dangerous place to freedom.

The promise feels more real, too: a land to work; a place where I belong; a setting where I can create, build, and grow something. That feels more compelling than the acquisition of right-opinion and a sense of superiority that comes from it.

What new harvest is happening in your life? How can you give back to God in gratitude?

TOTAL ENGAGEMENT
ROMANS 10:8b-13

Throughout our study of the lectionary selections of Paul's writings, it will be helpful to remember that Paul was a lot like me on Day One of my cross-country pilgrimage. He was sorting through several elements, all of them overlapping like a driver's thoughts and road awareness.

One was the faith that came suddenly to him on the road to Damascus. Without any warning or intellectual ground-laying, Paul found himself totally engaged with this Jesus whom he had been fighting. His entire being became caught up in Jesus.

A second was his work founding churches and mentoring the flawed but earnest leaders who were trying to establish Jesus-centered communities in a hostile environment. One moment, he was disappointed in them, and the next moment he was praising their good work. I sense that he wished they, too, could get totally engaged in Jesus.

A third element shaping Paul was the ongoing opposition that he and his fellow Christians were experiencing, especially within the Jewish community where they were initially a subgroup.

A fourth element was his desire to lay the intellectual ground for continuing church life. He was not a legalist or a theologian, but he did have certain ideas he hoped to plant among Christians, such as salvation by grace, not works.

It's like my drive on Day One of my 4,100-mile, 30-day pilgrimage, Fresh Day on the Road. I knew that first day would be difficult, because I would be making a number of transitions at the same time. I would transition from walking around San Mateo to driving two-lane roads. I would go from being with family to driving alone as a solo pilgrim. I would go from a place where I knew my way around to a journey in which I would very likely miss turns and select wrong roads. I would transition from walking and thinking without interruption to driving crowded roads with magnificent scenery and constant interruptions. Like Paul, I was leaving behind the world of the familiar and predictable, setting out on a journey where everything would be decidedly less clear-cut. I was called to be totally engaged with God while safely and successfully navigating the unknown road ahead.

In carrying out his complex agenda, Paul had an inherent limitation: He wasn't a very good writer. Actually, it's better to say that his skill as a writer was not commensurate with his passion and insight into Christian life and faith. He had some soaring moments, like his memorable words on love in 1 Corinthians 13, but mostly he struggled to convey his ideas. It's as if his vision outpaced his ability to find the right words to describe it. That's why people who read Paul literally and without digging into his ideas often fail to grasp his message.

In Romans 10:8b-13, Paul was trying to express the idea of total engagement. The word of God, Paul says, is near us, on our lips and in our heart (10:8 NRSV). Faith is a matter of head and heart, lips and life, expressing conviction and living that conviction. It isn't just intellectual assent or liturgical practice. It's giving oneself wholly to God. Proof of this total engagement, as Paul saw it, is the radical inclusion shown by believers. All who have this faith—expressing and living the conviction that Jesus is the resurrected Lord—are bound together by a common salvation. Because God is all in all, other distinctions like Jew versus Greek fade into insignificance (10:11-12).

We don't need to keep proving ourselves with proper practice. We just need to call on the name of the Lord (10:13). I don't think Paul was giving a formula for being saved. He was urging his friends to give everything to God. Christians have tended to use Paul as a key source for drafting the proper formula for "winning" and being "right." But such an interpretation misses Paul's deeper message: Don't hold back. Give your lips, your head, your heart, your tribal distinctions—your everything—to Jesus.

That giving of everything didn't happen for me on Day One of my pilgrimage. As I expected, my mind was too preoccupied to switch onto the track of deep reflection. I kept looking for turnouts where I could photograph vistas and double-check my route. I figured I was doing well to get onto the right roads for skirting below the Sierra Nevada range.

I felt scattered when I finally found a motel room in a land of few motels. Focus and deep thinking would have to come later. Like Paul, I was called and motivated to engage deeply with God. And if I couldn't find the focus for it right then, I just needed to be patient.

How is God challenging you to relinquish the familiar and take on something new?

IN THE WILDERNESS
LUKE 4:1-13

I'm sure it is no coincidence that I studied Jesus' temptation in the wilderness on the day I spent crossing the Mojave Desert in California. It's important to remember that as Luke describes Jesus' temptation, his details are rich with meaning. As I drove, I wondered what forty days alone in the Mojave would be like: just snakes and wild animals for company, no water, no food, no people, no break in the monotony. It would be just brown and dusty, probably hot in the day and cold at night.

Luke said God's Spirit led Jesus into the wilderness and kept him there for forty days, not unlike the Hebrews in their forty-year-long wilderness wandering from Egypt to Canaan (Luke 4:1-2). Perhaps even more meaningfully, Jesus' wilderness experience was not unlike the scapegoat of the Day of Atonement ritual, which was loaded down (figuratively) with Israel's sins and then led away into the wilderness (see Leviticus 16:20-22).

I have studied the story of Jesus' temptation many times and focused on the jousting between Jesus and the devil. This time, because of my crossing of the Mojave Desert, I saw deep meanings in the very setting itself. I think Luke wanted his readers to see Jesus totally alone, on the verge of collapse, and close to being broken. That is how wilderness experiences are for us. We use the term "wilderness" casually to describe any hard time. But there are places and there are experiences that go beyond challenging; they become excruciating, terrifying, soul-depleting, and spirit-breaking.

It is in those moments that the devil strikes. Not when we are having a bad day—though a bad day could make us vulnerable—but when everything is lost and we are aching in despair.

We need to see the difference. It is so easy to get caught up in so-called "first-world problems," like running out of seltzer, getting sass from a child, or being criticized at work. Those relatively minor difficulties can undo us. If unchecked, they can cause us to lash out at our partners, hit our children, or drown our sorrows in self-pity and booze.

Jesus was caught up in something altogether different, something we might never experience except for crushing losses like the death of a child or suffering a violent crime. Jesus showed an extraordinary ability to remember God even at a bottom that was below anything we know.

The evil one tested Jesus in three ways. They were, in effect, the three dreams people often have: magic, wealth and power, and equality with God.

First was the temptation for Jesus to turn a stone into a loaf of bread (Luke 4:3). Stone into bread, water into wine, bread into flesh, wine into blood—we have strong yearnings to do magic, to step outside the normal constraints of reality and do something supernatural. Think about it. How much of our modern worship or spirituality centers in a desire for magic, for escape into the supernatural?

Jesus responded that life isn't about what magic can produce—bread, in this instance—but about remaining faithful to God (Luke 4:4). It's not about jumping onto a different track where reality is suspended, but clinging to God in reality itself. In other words, in the morning watch as a parent, in the challenge of mastering lust and appetite, in turning down the terrible engine of self, we choose to stand with God. That is a lot more difficult than wishing upon a spiritual star that some magic moment will happen if we just yearn for it.

The second test was wealth and power. Satan promised Jesus what countless leaders, employers, and seducers have promised us: If we will just give ourselves to the tempter, we will have everything we want in life (Luke 4:5-7). Like an employer claiming to offer a boundless future of riches and applause, the devil claimed to control all that matters in life. The devil lied, of course.

We are surrounded by marketers and sellers with potent tools of persuasion. They promise us happiness, beauty, great sex, long life, and victory over our neighbors if we will just buy their product or give them our time and loyalty. They, too, lie.

Jesus responded by saying our loyalty should be to God. We worship and serve God alone (Luke 4:8). Whether you then become happy or beautiful or successful is beside the point. Faith isn't a tool for having our needs met or our desires fulfilled. Faith is its own reward. Knowing God is its own reward.

The third test promised equality with God if Jesus would simply test God and prove God's protection. By forcing God to protect him, Jesus could manipulate God into acting. Do you hear echoes of a common attitude toward prayer, mission, and stewardship? If I just pray hard enough, God will do my bidding. If I serve enough, God will shower me with blessings. If I give generously enough, God will favor me over others.

These are the deals that hubris makes. We demand that God abandon God's own name, which means "I will be who I will be," and accept our name for God, which would be "I will do what you ask me to do" (see Exodus 3:13-15).

Jesus responded that we must not put God to such a test (Luke 4:12). It is we who submit to God, adapt to God, and listen for God's bidding.

On my drive across the Mojave I heard the smooth sounds of seduction. First came a radio preacher outside Barstow, California, who vilified "unbelievers and liberals" as if the two were synonymous. Their failing was not taking the Bible literally, specifically in reference to the ability of snakes to talk. He sounded self-assured and had a pleasing voice.

The second was a pair of Fox News commentators on television at the Wagon Wheel restaurant in Needles, California. They were heaping scorn on President Obama for his initiative in fighting the Islamic State. They did their best to sound like experts speaking wisdom on military strategy, foreign affairs, and politics.

These words were spoken within self-contained bubbles, to use a modern idiom, taking no account of outside perspectives. There was no recognition that people who lean politically left might have an authentic experience of God, or that the Bible may contain a deeper meaning than surface-level details about the behaviors of ancient snakes. There was no acknowledgment that foreign policy and military strategy are complex issues with no clear, simple answers. Within those bubbles, everything could make sense and have the ring of truth.

In the wilderness, the devil testing Jesus was trying to create a similar bubble, in which all phenomena of the larger world faded away and all that remained was the pain of hunger and the smooth seduction of a self-assured liar claiming to speak all truth.

Truly difficult times often leave us in such a bubble. The waiting room outside critical care at a hospital, for example, becomes its own world. The family dealing with grief at home can feel cut off from other people. So can someone who has recently lost a job. When an addict attempts sobriety, it is critical that he or she not try to do it alone but in the company of other addicts in recovery. Those in recovery well know the danger of being isolated in their own bubble.

This Gospel reading, you see, isn't just a quaint story from the mythological prehistory of Jesus. It connects directly with the worlds we know, and its message is clear: When times are tough—as they inevitably will be—the evil one tries to draw us inside a bubble where we lose touch with reality. In such times we must remember with renewed dedication to worship God, cling to God, listen to God, and serve God alone.

In all three settings described in today's readings—Israel starting its life in Canaan, Paul entering the total-engagement phase of his apostolic ministry, and Jesus making the transition from his baptism to active ministry—God's people were a work in progress. They were just starting out, making a fresh response to God's call, probably with little or no idea of what lay ahead.

This is our connection with them. Some of us have more religious experience than others, but I suspect we are all, in our own way, just getting started in trying to be God's people in the world. As we do, it is important to keep a few things in mind.

First, we must recognize what new harvest is happening our lives. God brings us to new land and shows us new light. In the case of the Hebrews, they were laying the fruits of their agricultural work before God. Think beyond grain and livestock. Think the paycheck you earn, the skills you are developing, the legacy you are forming in the day-to-day of work. Some of this will be new. What is that newness? Can you see how God has given it to you?

Second, if you are seeking to be responsive to God, then you will inevitably be facing a new, perhaps challenging, level of engagement. That means letting go of former things and hearing God's fresh call. It means transformation as a person, not just new assignments as a church worker. What does God seem to be challenging you to relinquish and to take on?

Third, the transition from a baptismal faith to a total life-in-God faith is huge. A baptismal faith starts you on the course of new life, gives you new "garments," as it were, and a new identity as a follower of Jesus Christ. A total life-in-God faith presses back against the ways of this world, especially the seductions. You don't just self-identify as a Christian. You take on the suffering servanthood of Jesus, the moral

THE GIFT OF NEW CREATION

clarity of Jesus, the risks of speaking truth to power, and the likelihood that many will push back and hurt you. Do you see any of this risk and pushback happening in your life? If so, where are you gaining strength to press onward? If not, where are you holding back so as to avoid risk and wound?

What does the wilderness look and feel like in your life?

GROUP STUDY GUIDE

Questions for Discussion

1. Can you identify a moment or turning point in your life that you would characterize as "liberation from bondage"?

2. How do you personally show gratitude for that liberation?

3. What new harvest has God given you, and how is God calling you to respond to it?

4. Name an area of your life in which God is calling you to "total engagement." What would it mean for you to become more deeply engaged with God in this area?

5. In the Lord's Prayer we ask God to "lead us not into temptation," or, in the NRSV translation of Luke 11:4, "do not bring us to the time of trial." These variants refer both to the wilderness wandering of the Hebrews after the Exodus and to Jesus being tested by Satan in the wilderness. How did God save the Hebrews and Jesus from these times of temptation?

6. Which of the temptations described above—magic, wealth and power, or equality with God—do you find most difficult to resist? Why?

7. Are you aware of any times when God has put you to the test? How did you deal with these circumstances?

8. What would you tell someone else facing the wilderness?

Suggestions for Group Study

Share Your Faith Story

Each of us has a faith story to tell. All are different—no one of us knows all truth—and all faith stories matter, even those that some find shallow or off-the-wall. Form pairs, and ask each person to share his or her faith story with his or her partner. Allow time for both partners to share. If pairs or individuals struggle to tell their faith stories, the following questions may serve as helpful prompts:

How did you first come to know God?

When is a time you have felt close to God?

How has your spiritual life changed over time?

How is God working in your life right now?

Conclude the time in pairs by asking the partners to pray together, taking turns giving thanks for the other person's faith journey and asking God to continue walking with them.

When each pair has finished sharing and praying, gather the whole group back together and discuss the following questions:

Why is it important to tell our faith stories to one another?

What is the relationship between our personal faith stories and the story of God's people in the Bible?

Break Out of the Bubbles

In the center of a markerboard, chalkboard, or large piece of paper, write the word *wilderness*. Ask group members to identify situations in which they have experienced the wilderness as described above, times of loneliness, isolation, and vulnerability that felt like rock bottom. Alternatively, they can imagine such situations as possibilities if they have not had many such experiences.

As group members respond, write each situation on the board or paper, drawing a bubble around it to signify isolation. Next, discuss each bubble in turn, focusing on how the bubble's limitations can cause doubt, despair, or faulty thinking. What does each self-contained bubble cut off from the outside? What temptations are especially dangerous in each bubble? What will it take to break out of those bubbles and see God and other people from a broader, more authentic perspective?

Conclude the conversation by addressing this question: What bubble or bubbles might our local community or congregation be living in without realizing it? What are we missing as a result?

Closing Prayer

O God, help me to be more than a cultural Christian. Help me to be a follower of Jesus: a doer of things he did, a confident wanderer to a new land, a person ready for total engagement and bold in the wilderness of temptation. Help me to venture beyond what I know and go to challenging places in search of you. Amen.

A Cause for Lament

Scriptures for the
Second Sunday of Lent
Genesis 15:1-12, 17-18
Philippians 3:17–4:1
Luke 13:31-35

My reflection on this week's lessons has been deeply influenced by my sobering, disturbing encounter with the Navajo Nation and what white people did to them one hundred and fifty years ago.

My people—my people! my ancestors! all church-going Christians!—took land that belonged others. They claimed a divinely written destiny that required the land to be theirs. But that was just a way of dressing up greed.

The Europeans who colonized this land wanted the New World to be a blank slate where we could build a "city on a hill." But it wasn't a blank slate. Nor were we a blank slate as people. The land had inhabitants, and some of them, like the Cherokee, were more civilized than we were. And our European heritage had left us burdened with our own sins and flaws.

The Scriptures for this week remind us to be careful as we lay claim to our spiritual heritage. As history has shown time and time again, we become tyrants when we grasp for God's promises with little regard for others who might be affected. As you read the lessons for this second week of Lent, look through a different lens and consider the following: The land God promised to Abram and his offspring belonged to someone else first. It still belonged to someone else when the Hebrews took possession of it after coming out of Egypt. The same is true for the spiritual landscape that new Christians wanted to inhabit in the days of the early church. And the same is true for the city of Jerusalem, which had become corrupted in Jesus' day.

None of these was a blank slate. Rather, in each case God was doing something new with things that were old. A humble and God-centered approach to that newness would have considered the price that others were paying and wondered how old and new could coexist in mutual respect. All too often, the new occupants treated their predecessors as enemies. God's gift of the land to Abram became the rationale for the extermination of the Canaanites in Deuteronomy and Joshua. Paul and Jesus show us a better way. In Philippians, Paul describes "enemies of the cross" with deep sadness, recognizing that their destruction is something to be mourned rather than celebrated. And as Jesus laments over Jerusalem, he calls out the corruption of the city that had become too enamored with its own power and glory.

Much of world history emerges from the tension between these two possible responses of triumphalism and mutual respect. Far too often, history has followed the path of destruction. Those who have claimed to be God's people have ended up doing little better than the US Army troops who uprooted the Navajo from their land so that whites could have it.

Much of our faith world flows from that tension, as well. Today's readings are a sobering reminder that we must choose respect, lest we become tyrants acting in the name of God.

THE LAND
GENESIS 15:1-12, 17-18

As I drove north on US 89 from Flagstaff, Arizona, and then East on US 160 into the Navajo Nation and the Hopi Reservation, I found the land less desolate than the Mojave Desert west of Kingman, but still barren.

"Why would anyone want this land?" I thought—quite foolishly, I admit. The answer, of course, is that this is tribal land. It is their land. It doesn't matter that my sense of land has been shaped by Indiana's fertile farmland, Carolina's rich clay, and New York's concrete world. These 27,425 square miles in three states are where the United States Government settled the Navajo Nation in the 1860s, with another 2,532 square miles belonging to the Hopi.

The Navajo Nation is the largest Native American reservation in the United States. It has its own judicial, law-making, and law enforcement

THE GIFT OF NEW CREATION

systems, and it is functionally separate from the surrounding states of Arizona, Utah, and New Mexico. The land belonging to the Navajo Nation might be impoverished in many ways, but it is their land.

If I had stopped in Tuba City, Arizona, for several days, I would have learned to rue my initial question. Even on my first day there, I sensed the beauty and vitality of the red land with its rugged terrain and wind-shaped stone formations. My point is that people need land, and their land needn't be perfect, as someone else might measure perfection. It needs to be theirs.

The call of Abraham turns on the matter of land. Abram, as he was originally named, first heard God's call in Genesis 12, where God beckoned him to leave behind his home and family and depart "for the land that I will show you" (Genesis 12:1). Though he was following God's lead, the experience surely was unsettling for Abram. It must have felt in some ways like the Navajo being forced to give up their ancient homeland and travel to a new place. Abram obeyed, and when he arrived in Canaan God gave the land to him and his offspring: "I give this land to your descendants" (Genesis 12:7). The unseen, foreign land to which he traveled became his possession, the heritage of all those who would later claim Abram as their ancestor.

In today's passage, we see Abram's faith in God's promise begin to waver. When God promises him that "your reward will be very great" (Genesis 15:1), Abram questions the usefulness of a gift that will leave his family when he dies without any offspring. Abram is old, and his possessions will become the property of a man named Eliezer of Damascus when he dies (Genesis 15:2-3). What can God possibly give Abram, he asks, since he has no children (Genesis 15:2)?

God repeats that Abram will become the father of a great nation, with biological descendants as numerous as the stars. Old as he is, Abram will have a son who will inherit the land that God has promised (Genesis 15:4-5). And in a profound demonstration of faith, Abram believes God: "Abram trusted the LORD, and the LORD recognized Abram's high moral character" (Genesis 15:6). With the question of Abram's offspring settled for now, God makes a covenant with Abram, promising to give his descendants the land of Canaan (Genesis 15:18).

Abram (Abraham) eventually became the father of Isaac, who became the father of Jacob, also known as Israel. Jacob was the father of twelve sons, who became the ancestors of the twelve tribes of Israel.

They became a great nation, and eventually possessed the land that God promised to Abram.

We see this mythological drama from a great distance, and it seems lofty. The day-to-day reality of it probably was less exalted. Sarah and her mistress Hagar vied for status; Hagar and her son Ishmael were driven away; and Isaac's sons Jacob and Esau clashed again and again. And all the while, the land remained the property of someone else. If we read on through the next couple of verses past today's passage, we see that the land promised to Abram belonged at the time to a diverse collection of local peoples: the Kenites, Kenizzites, Kadmonites, Hittites, Perizzites, Rephaim, Amorites, Canaanites, Girgashites, and Jebusites (Genesis 15:19-20).

We would do well to remember that Abram did not receive an uninhabited piece of land. It was no blank slate, but God doing something new in the midst of something old.

The day-to-day reality of the "rez," as the Navajo reservation is known, is no less gritty. In a wandering drive around the area, I saw the grim signs of poverty: dilapidated houses, many boarded up; too many people sharing too little space; old cars lined up outside; rutted dirt roads even in the city; and a downscale array of stores.

Seen from a distance, however, the Navajo Nation and the Hopi rez that it surrounds seem to inspire pride. I wonder what new thing God might be doing there.

What new thing is God doing in your life? What might it be costing someone else?

CROSSROADS
PHILIPPIANS 3:17–4:1

Four Corners, USA, is a monument to surveyors and maps.

It is the place where the borders of four states—Arizona, New Mexico, Colorado, and Utah—come together, as if perfectly squared puzzle pieces had been laid in alignment. Boundary decisions made in Washington under President Lincoln and implemented by surveyors played out in a single spot where, for a $5 admission fee, you can stand and be in all four states at once.

The spot itself is located inside a square amphitheater whose outside walls are set aside for Native Americans from each state to sell turquoise, beaded, and silver jewelry. If you walk outside the booth area, you can see each state in succession. They all look alike—maps don't determine geology, after all—which I found unsettling. Without this monument inscribing four lines emanating from a central spot, you would not know you were looking at, say, Utah and not New Mexico.

The monument must be quite absurd to the Navajo Nation, whose large reservation spills into all four states, paying no attention to state boundaries. The frybread sold here is Navajo frybread, and that's that. A monument to maps and borders is white man's stuff, not theirs.

There is a significant parallel between the intersecting lines at Four Corners and Paul's exhortation to the church at Philippi in Philippians in 3:17–4:1. In a sense, the new Christians were rearranging the very land on which their people had long walked. They were looking beyond accepted borders, seeing God in new ways, and giving their allegiance to an itinerant rabbi named Jesus who had no home. They took this border-smashing behavior with them as they spread into the larger Mediterranean world. Whether the old ways were Jewish, Roman, or Greek, the new Christians largely ignored them. They were standing on a new point in a new moment. In his inauguration of God's kingdom, Jesus had given them a new map with which to understand the world, and Paul was helping them to navigate it.

Instead of following Moses, they were to imitate Paul, one who had witnessed the risen Christ and embraced Christ's sufferings in his own person (Philippians 3:17). Instead of obeying the Law, they were following the example of Paul. Instead of seeing all other people as unclean, the new Christians distinguished between "enemies of the cross" and citizens of heaven (Philippians 3:18-20). Like the map point at Four Corners, Paul drew clear lines of distinction. He described the enemies this way: "Their lives end with destruction. Their god is their stomach, and they take pride in their disgrace because their thoughts focus on earthly things" (Philippians 3:19). That description, of course, is a resume for worldly success, including the power to oppress the Christians. Paul assured his beloved friends in Philippi that God would transform their humiliation into glory, if only they would "stand firm in the Lord" (Philippians 4:1).

Reality tends to be fuzzy. It's hard to know what you are looking at sometimes. But Paul, in effect, urged Christians to keep referring to the center (himself, and through him Jesus). They were to imitate him, just as he imitated Jesus. Paul strived to place the cross at the center of his life, and he called the Philippians to do the same. It's not lost on me that the intersecting lines at Four Corners create the shape of a cross. The lines radiating from the center might go in different directions, just as the churches established by Paul and others took different courses in creating their fellowships. What binds the lines is the cross at the center. Not the vendors standing around the outside selling products to convert a scenic moment into commerce, but the center itself. And what binds the Christian communities together is the cross of Christ, which stands at the center of their common life and hope.

When I drove away from the Four Corners monument, I had a choice to make: Turn left toward Utah and Colorado, or right toward Arizona and New Mexico. I turned right. That turn soon brought me to another choice: Go back west the way I came, or turn left toward New Mexico. There followed more choices, and then more choices after that. Each choice put other possibilities aside until I was many miles from that center point defined by surveyors.

Our Hebrew ancestors would say that my journey actually began at the Pacific Ocean, just as theirs began in Egypt. From a driving standpoint that is correct. But I saw at Four Corners a moment where everything was possible: four states, and beyond each one other states, other tribes, other stories. It was sobering to realize that from that center I had to make fundamental choices. Each choice I made would close out other possibilities. I needed a reference point: an overarching goal (to reach the Hudson River Valley) and a hope (to see new things along the way).

Jesus is our central point. All things become possible in him. Then, as we live into our calling and choose the road map we will follow, some possibilities fade away, and new choices emerge.

What choices have you made, and how have they affected your future?

THE POWER OF LAMENT
LUKE 13:31-35

The two saddest phrases in the Bible, in my opinion, are when God cried out to Adam and Eve in the garden, "Where are you?" and these words of lament from Luke 13:34: "Jerusalem, Jerusalem!" Jesus echoes David's grieving cry, "Absalom! Oh, Absalom!" after his son was killed during an unsuccessful bid to usurp the throne of Israel.

Behavior has consequences. Those consequences hurt people, and the hurt of those people hurts God. That's the great mystery we face: a God who suffers with us, on behalf of us, and because of us.

Jesus' cry for Jerusalem is a lament. After three days of driving through Native American reservations in Arizona and New Mexico, seeing the great price these native peoples paid for the greed and cruelty of whites, this seems to me to be a good occasion for hearing laments.

Whites took the good farmland owned by native tribes and gave them back barren desert, where they cannot grow crops, graze cattle, or find jobs. Many natives leave the reservations and go to more prosperous communities like Farmington, New Mexico, and assimilate, even intermarry. Many of those who stay on tribal land live in poverty not unlike the poverty that coal miners have had to endure in the hollows of Appalachia and migrant farmworkers in California and North Carolina.

I don't know if the Navajo people are sad. But I felt sad. I felt a lament rising within me. I saw the injustice. I read about the "Long Walk" of 1864 when the US Army forced the Navajo to leave their land and walk three hundred miles to the west, which many didn't survive. When they were allowed to return four years later, they came back to a much diminished piece of land—essentially land for which whites couldn't find a profitable use. I read about the Army man who shot a pregnant Navajo woman because she had gone into labor and was slowing them down.

I felt anger rising within me, as well as shame at the white-power excesses perpetrated by my ancestors throughout American history. A lament, you see, is more than sadness. It's anger, and it's frustration. It's an awareness of betrayal.

Jesus had no illusions about Herod, the ruler of Galilee where Jesus conducted much of his ministry. He knew "that fox" was an enemy, intent on his destruction. But when Jesus thought of Jerusalem—the city David built up as an offering to God and then sullied with his lust, the city ruled by unjust kings and self-serving priests, the city that invaders sacked, the city where a corrupt temple cult wanted this Messiah Jesus to fail—Jesus felt the bitterness that God feels, a bitterness fed by a yearning for something better.

Jesus likened himself to a hen aching to protect her brood but discovering that her children aren't willing. In effect, this one image summed up the Hebrew and human relationship with God from Adam and Eve to the Messiah himself.

"Your house is abandoned," Jesus said (Luke 13:35). The first readers of Luke's Gospel, of course, knew exactly what happened to that "house." The Romans destroyed the Temple in Jerusalem some thirty to forty years after Jesus died. It must have grieved Jesus to know that Jerusalem would be destroyed. It grieved him even more to know that Jerusalem and its people would put him to death, rejecting the very one who came to save them.

Jesus knew that the result of traveling to Jerusalem was inevitable. The city had a history of killing prophets (Luke 13:34). He would arrive on the day we call Palm Sunday, to the joyful praise of the people. But less than a week later, the people would immediately turn against him. And so on his way to Jerusalem, Jesus raises a lament for the city, expressing his anger and frustration and, yes, sadness.

The power of the lament is its transparency. The lament reveals one's hurt and sadness, one's regret at something being lost. Laments often don't get resolved. They just get voiced. In that voicing, one takes the risk of vulnerability, bearing one's troubled self to others. One opens oneself to the risk of having the lament be rejected, ridiculed, or ignored.

I think laments have gone out of fashion. We understand grief, depression, and sadness, and we understand remorse and regret. The lament includes those elements, but it also incorporates something more. It includes an appeal to God, a statement of one's innocence, a curse on the one causing pain, an expression of confidence that God will act, and a song of thanksgiving. It does all those in a somewhat lyrical manner, as a song perhaps.

Luke's audience would have understood Jesus' words as a lament, such as what we see in some of the Psalms. The distress Jesus expressed wasn't his awareness of the forces gathering against him. The distress was how his people were behaving. He saw that the great drama of the Hebrew Bible had come down to this: weak people easily manipulated by the establishment, crying praise of Jesus and then just as quickly demanding his death. The liberation from bondage in Egypt, the creation of the nation, the building of a Temple, and the return from exile had been reduced to this tragic display.

All of this week's lessons lead up to Jesus' lament over Jerusalem, a city formed for greatness that had become a reminder of all the compromises God's people had made over many centuries, all the ways they had disappointed God. Life doesn't end when we fail God. We might even think we have gotten away with something, or maybe that we have been smarter than God. But sins accumulate, and until we ask God to remove them from us, the burden just gets heavier and heavier and our behavior becomes worse and worse.

Early Americans got away with slavery, which denied basic humanity to a race of people and used them for economic gain. They applied that same denial and exploitation to Native Americans. Whites got rich on the backs of slaves, and other whites took the land of the Cherokee, Seminole, and others and sent them off to die on long marches. An entire society was grounded in brutal treatment of vulnerable minorities.

Modern Americans resent being tarred with those brushes. But that's the problem Jesus faced in Jerusalem. Until people confess their sins and the sins of their ancestors, until we root out and cease the behaviors of yesterday, yesterday stays alive. Slavery leads to civil war leads to reconstruction leads to the Klan leads to Jim Crow laws leads to bombings leads to shootings of unarmed black men.

This will seem harsh to many. But that, in my opinion, is precisely where Jesus' lament over Jerusalem leads. God wants more from us than a blind eye toward our own history. God wants repentance and new life.

The question for us, then, is what history we are holding on to and refusing to turn over to God in sincere repentance. It isn't enough to count the years between 1838 and now, or to dispute any attitudinal link to misbehaving ancestors. New start means new start. What new starts are you engaged in?

As you look at the world around you, where are you moved to lament? What new start can you make in response?

GROUP STUDY GUIDE

Questions for Discussion

1. Read Abram's story carefully, and identify where your life intersects with his most directly. In the possession or promise of land? In the call to follow God into the unknown? In facing an uncertain future? In some other way? What lesson can you learn from Abram's story?

2. What did Abram have to sacrifice in order to follow God? What did he gain in return?

3. What have you had to sacrifice in order to follow God and live out your faith? What have you gained in return?

4. What stands at the center of Paul's life in Christ, the anchor point that enables him to make sense of everything else?

5. In what way does this same center point define our life together today?

6. In your own life, who has served as an example for you to imitate? Have you served as a good example for someone else?

7. What does Jesus' lament for Jerusalem reveal about God? How would you have responded to Jesus if you were one of his followers and had heard his words about Jerusalem?

8. What might move Jesus to a similar lament in our world today?

Suggestions for Group Study

Compose a Group Lament

As the reflection above indicates, a song or psalm of lament provides a point of comparison for Jesus' cry of distress for Jerusalem. The CEB Study Bible identifies three main components of a psalm of lament: a description of trouble or complaint, a petition to God for help, and an expression of trust or praise (*The CEB Study Bible* pages 837-838 OT). Jesus' words correspond to the first part, a description of distress or trouble, namely the bad fate that characterizes Jerusalem.

As a group, identify one situation in today's world that seems to you to be a cause for lament. This could be something in your congregation, in your local community, or something tragic or difficult in the world at large. Form three teams, and ask each team to write one part of a lament psalm to express how your group feels about this situation and ask for God's guidance.

The first team should write a description of the trouble, giving expression to what is wrong, why it's wrong, and the sadness, anger, or distress that arises as a result of this.

The second team should write a prayer asking God to intervene, petitioning God to rectify the situation.

The third team should write an expression of confidence and trust in God, giving voice to the assurance that God can and will intercede and set things right.

As a variation on this exercise, groups may write their portions in a liturgical call-and-response format, alternating between a leader reading one line and the entire group reading a line in response.

Gather the whole group back together after these portions have been completed, and ask one volunteer from each team to read their portion of the lament. Discuss what emotions, thoughts, and desires arose in each team as they wrote their portion.

Conclude this exercise by putting the whole lament psalm together and praying it aloud as a group.

Map the Crossroads

Give each group member a blank sheet of paper and a pen or pencil. Ask each person to spend a few quiet moments thinking back across his or her life and identify "center points," moments in time that were rich with possibility and many choices. What have been the crossroads in your life where you could have gone in any one of many possible directions? Possible answers might include graduating from high school, moving to a new city, choosing a life partner, or beginning a new job.

Ask group members to use these center points to draw a map of their lives, tracking the string of choices that connected each of the center points to each other and led group members to where they are now. Group members should pay attention to the choices they made, the possibilities that were fully realized, the possibilities that were left behind, and the new possibilities that arose as a result of each choice.

After members have finished drawing their maps, have each member share his or her map with the group, being mindful that some may prefer not to share. Then discuss the following questions:

What led you to make the choices you made, to realize certain possibilities and not others?

Do you ever wonder how things would have been different if you had made a different choice? Why or why not?

Where along the way did God transform you and conform you to something good?

What possibilities exist where you are right now? What will it mean to realize one or some of these possibilities and leave others behind?

What reference point or goal can you uphold to help you make these decisions with no regrets?

Closing Prayer

O God, help me to look at all that I hold in my hands, and all that ties me down, and all that you have given me but I have squandered. Help me to see the ways I have disappointed you. Then give me the strength to choose life over death, freedom over bondage, service over safety. I seek a new start in you. Amen.

Learning to See As God Sees

Scriptures for the
Third Sunday of Lent
Isaiah 55:1-9
1 Corinthians 10:1-13
Luke 13:1-9

Crossing northeastern Arkansas was a far cry from the Hebrews crossing the Sinai wilderness or the Israelites crossing the desert on their way home from Babylon. The terrain was bleak and the poverty of towns was deep. But even there I had some warm experiences, like lunch with some local residents at a diner in Hardy, so it wasn't exactly what I'd call the wilderness. The Hebrews coming out of Egypt and the Israelites returning from Babylon had a harder time of it.

And yet, I still noticed a similarity between my journey and theirs. Like the post-exodus Hebrews and post-exilic Israelites, I had choices to make on how to live in this unfamiliar land. I could complain or listen; judge the bleak or celebrate the human; consider my time there empty, or find God within it; be glad I could pass the locals by, or hear the kindness in their voices.

The Scriptures this week offer three moments in a single journey, namely, the journey of submitting to the mind of God. No, as Isaiah said, God's ways aren't our ways. But our ways could be more like God's ways if we tried. Life tests us, and it is quite natural that we often fail those tests, Paul suggested. But we can try to live the way God has shown us, for God gives us mercy and time to do better. Like the gardener of Jesus' parable, God would rather cultivate our lives to produce fruit than uproot us and throw us away. As one of my favorite songs puts it, "You are a God of second chances. You bless and free us from the past."

In my case, I have tended too often to judge others as inadequate. That has hurt them and myself. I am learning to accept others as they are: not perfect, but no more imperfect than I am. Not exactly living God's way, but trying our best. If I want to live as God's person, then I had better try to see others God's way going forward.

So, no, northeastern Arkansas wasn't my favorite part of my 4,100-mile pilgrimage. I felt a lot more connected in other places, such as Enid, Oklahoma. But I learned something about God's ways in Mountain Home and Hardy. Those learnings, in turn, prepared me to accept my day at Camp Breckinridge, Kentucky, and wish in vain for more glimpses of my parents there.

HOPES AND EXPECTATIONS
ISAIAH 55:1-9

As I began my reflection on Isaiah's words, I had just entered the tenth town of my cross-country drive. The town was Mountain Home, Arkansas, a town with a great name at least.

I had experienced ten towns, ten hotel rooms, ten arrivals filled with expectation and hope. I didn't put my expectations and hopes into words each time. I just know I looked around eagerly, hoping to find something that resonated, stirred my thinking, maybe even inspired me. I knew not to look for a Manhattan sidewalk or a glimpse of some city where I have lived. Each town is unique. Each town, even the most meager, surely has happy spots as well as sad spots, uplifting vistas as well as down-at-the-heels stretches. Coming into a new town is a bit like going on a blind date. You hope for the best. No matter how many times you have been disappointed, you hope for the best.

Imagine the Hebrews making their long and anxious way from Babylon home to Zion. The people of Judah had been exiled to Babylon in 587 B.C., after their Temple and the city of Jerusalem had been conquered and destroyed. Now, some fifty years later, they were returning to Jerusalem where they could rebuild. That is the background for Isaiah Chapters 40–66: The people were going home. At least, the prophet said it was their home. Most of these exiles had never seen it. Half a century had passed since the people of Judah arrived in Babylon. A generation had died and a new one had been born. They had grown up in a strange land. All but the oldest of them were coming to Jerusalem and the countryside of their history as strangers, seeing it for the first time.

What would these people need to hear from the prophet who proclaimed their liberty and called them out of Babylon (see Isaiah 40)? This is what the prophet's words in Chapter 55 are all about. It's God's promise of what lies ahead.

They will find water! After this dreary wilderness, they will move beyond thirst. They will have abundance! Even if they have "no money," they will eat and be filled.

It will be free! God will provide for their needs even if they cannot pay. Besides, what God promises them is beyond price. Unlike things they once could buy but found didn't satisfy, God will provide food that is "good," the "richest of feasts" (Isaiah 55:1-2).

Thus far, this sounds like coming home to a welcoming parent after a long time away. Walk in the door, and sit down to eat. No questions asked.

But there is more. Isaiah says God will make an "everlasting covenant" with them (Isaiah 55:3). It will be like the covenant God made with David during Israel's heyday. They will become a great nation once again, and other nations will be drawn to them because theirs is the one true God. Even nations that are strange to you, and you to them, will "run to you," Isaiah says (verse 5).

What should the returning exiles do in return? "Seek the LORD when he can still be found" (Isaiah 55:6). This is a pregnant moment. God is open to you; all things are open to you. Don't waste it. The wicked must give up their wicked ways and the unrighteous their unrighteous thoughts. You have been set free from bondage. Live now as a new people, freed from your former ways. God has promised to "have mercy" on you if you repent (Isaiah 55:7).

Maybe this makes no sense to the people. No other god is like this. No other people are like this. But such is the nature of your God. God's ways aren't like your ways. God's thoughts aren't like your thoughts (Isaiah 55:8-9 NRSV).

In these nine verses, Isaiah gives a promise of great meaning. It fulfills every expectation and hope: water, food, respect, and a God who is eager to embrace and be embraced. Yet it is also a call to live differently. God wasn't bringing the people home from Babylon in order to resume former ways. They couldn't live as they had in Babylon, and they couldn't live as their ancestors had done in Jerusalem. It was a new start. The message is challenging: If all they do is resume life as the previous generation knew it, all the blessings will be lost.

Good food requires good behavior. And it requires eyes to see as God does, to recognize the abundance and promise of Zion and the call to receive it with a new way of life.

There I was in a strange town called Mountain View. As I looked around, I admit I did not have high expectations. But that was an old way of seeing the world. I needed to accept it for what it was and seek out the beauty that could be found. That was my challenge before I pressed on down the road toward the Mississippi River. I needed to see with God's eyes and discover the abundance that was there. Instead of going through a mental checklist—remember the blind date analogy—I was charged to accept the small city as it was. Did I see any familiar markers, like a Starbucks, a western wear store, or a barbecue joint? Maybe not, but it didn't matter. God's ways aren't our ways. In order to see more of what God shows us, we must often abandon what we might consider normal.

God always has more to show us than we are willing to see.

How can you shape your expectations and hopes to fit God's desire for you?

LEARNING FROM THE PAST
1 CORINTHIANS 10:1-13

On my drive across northeastern Arkansas, I took a side trip into the small town of Hardy, with a population of 712. I found a main street of stores designed to catch the summer tourist trade. Most were closed on a bitter cold day in February.

One restaurant was open. I was their only customer until a couple walked in. I asked the waitress to tell me about Hardy. She didn't know much, but the retired couple who came in after me knew a lot. The wife's family has been in that town for a century. She gave me a word-picture view of the town as it used to be. She told me about the big house down the road where a woman used to raise guinea hens as her protection against intruders. She told me about where the high school used to be, as well as several stores.

Nowadays, Hardy has a small part of Arkansas' abundant summer water-recreation business. The main activity in town comes from long trains hauling coal from North Dakota to Memphis through the center of town. The couple and I talked across the otherwise vacant restaurant for thirty minutes. It was great. So was the food. You never know what the journey will bring.

Paul saw the church in Corinth as people on a journey. In this chapter of his letter, he drew an extended comparison between their experience and the Hebrews' crossing of the wilderness after the exodus from Egypt. His point in doing so was that these Christians should understand the tests that the Hebrews faced and failed and learn from them how to avoid failing their own tests.

He used imagery from Christian liturgy to start the comparison. The Hebrews themselves had walked under the cloud of God's Holy Spirit and been "baptized" in the waters of the Reed Sea (1 Corinthians 10:1-2). They, too, had eaten spiritual food and drink (as in the Eucharist). They, too, had drawn sustenance from the "rock," a reference to a legend about a rock that traveled with them, which Paul understood as the presence of the preexistent Christ (verses 3-4).

Paul then issued his warning. The Hebrews lost God's favor and perished in the wilderness, as did Moses in punishment for the people's sins. Paul told them exactly how the Hebrews went astray. They became idolaters, crafting a golden calf to worship (see Exodus 32). Don't worship false gods, Paul said (1 Corinthians 10:7).

Despite the command not to worship other gods, the Hebrews worshiped the Moabites' god after many of them had sexual relations with the women of Moab. In anger at their behavior, God sent a plague to put the violators to death, some 24,000 in all (see Numbers 25:1-9). Don't engage in immorality, Paul said (1 Corinthians 10:8).

The Hebrews "became impatient" and complained against God and against Moses for bringing them to this harsh place where they had no food or water. God punished them by sending serpents that bit them and caused many to die (see Numbers 21:4-6). Don't test Christ, Paul said (1 Corinthians 10:9).

The Hebrews repeatedly turned against Moses and grumbled, accusing him of lying about leading them to a Promised Land flowing with milk and honey. Instead, they charged, Moses intended to kill them in the wilderness. Time and again God punished them, including the time God sent a plague to kill 14,700 of them before Aaron performed an act of atonement for the people (see Numbers 16:41-49). Don't turn against God, Paul said—or by extension, against Paul (1 Corinthians 10:10).

These events in the wilderness happened as an example for Christians, Paul wrote to the Corinthians. No matter how righteous they thought themselves, they must realize that they, too, could "fall" when the testing comes. Paul exhorted them to trust God to be faithful, testing them only with what they could endure and providing them a way forward (1 Corinthians 10:11-13). Paul was likening the Christians in their trials to the Hebrews in the wilderness. God was faithful then, and God will be faithful now. Jesus the "rock" was with the Hebrews, and he will be with his chosen people now.

One of the hardest aspects of being a twenty-first-century Christian is that, in the West at least, claiming Jesus and following him aren't likely to lead to suffering. We might be ignored, but probably not persecuted. And yet the tests and trials facing us are real. And they are similar to those that led both the Hebrews and the Corinthians astray. Pride, for example, afflicted them, and it afflicts us. Like them, we too are given to shallow faith that cannot endure difficulties. Our society has its own brands of sexual immorality, such as an epidemic of adultery or the sexual abuse of children and women. We are tempted to devote ourselves to other gods, called wealth or success rather than Ba'al but no less a competitor for our allegiance to God. We too turn on our designated leaders, crave power, pursue comfort, and foster divisions among the faithful. All of these things happen in their own way today, just as they happened in the wilderness and in Corinth.

Paul's message is as important for us as it was for the Corinthians. He is saying that for all of the grand liturgies we create, for all the right opinions we espouse, for all the institutional success we have or want to have, we can lose it all by turning against God. On our journey, we must recognize our tests and not think ourselves incapable of falling. God wants us to be as steadfast for God as God is for us.

What temptations do you face?

THE SMALL PICTURE
LUKE 13:1-9

When I crossed the Mississippi River into Tennessee, my original plan was to dawdle my way to Eastern Tennessee and visit a friend near Knoxville, and perhaps hunker down for two or three days in a cabin he owns.

But when I looked at the road map, I realized that turning north toward Morganfield, Kentucky, was important to me. There I would find what remains of Camp Breckinridge, an Army training and POW center where my parents were stationed during World War II. Indeed, it was there that I was conceived and spent my first year or so as a baby. Most of the Camp Breckinridge's thirty-six thousand acres have since reverted to farmland, with eight hundred acres set aside for a Job Corps site plus a small parcel on which a former center for non-commissioned officers serves as a museum.

My parents didn't talk much about their war years. I know my dad was proud to serve and, as newlyweds, they found ways to make the best of it. When it appeared certain that Hitler was going down, they felt confident about starting a family.

I wasn't prepared, therefore, for the vast scope of Camp Breckinridge. Its population peaked at fifty-five thousand, the size of a small city. It had eighteen hundred buildings, a full array of training facilities for infantry and airborne, and a prison for housing close to four thousand German prisoners of war, most captured in North Africa.

Military bases like this one were built across the country during the war. Hundreds of them held POWs, including four bases in Kentucky, fourteen in Nebraska, and thirty-five in Texas. The war effort, in other words, was far more vast than I had imagined. It engaged the entire country and touched virtually every aspect of life. And yet, as vast as the war was, every soldier was someone's son or daughter, and every loss was felt deeply. From a personal perspective, this was a small-lens war: my father, his duty, my pride, his patriotism. All vast movements come down to personal stories.

I think of this as I read the Gospel reading for the third week of Lent: Jesus' words on repentance, as recorded in Luke 13:1-9. Using contemporary events as examples, Jesus dealt with the question of deserved or undeserved suffering. Religious leaders tended to explain suffering as God's punishment for sins. Did that mean the Galileans executed by Pilate while sacrificing in the Temple were unusually abhorrent sinners (Luke 13:1-2)? Or those who were crushed by a falling tower, were they "more guilty of wrongdoing than everyone else who lives in Jerusalem" (verse 4)?

That "macro" question—looking at the whole array of human consequences—misses the point, said Jesus. The point is what happens in individual lives. If people repent, God will forgive them. If they don't repent, people will bring suffering upon themselves. The intersection of grace, mercy, sin, and human responsibility comes down to repentance, that is, when one individual confesses to God and changes his or her heart and life.

To underscore the point about individual repentance, Jesus went on to tell about a single fig tree planted in a single vineyard. It was bearing no fruit, so the owner wanted to cut it down. The gardener, however, bargained for time. Give the tree one more season, he said to the owner, and I will tend it carefully. If, after a year, it still is bearing no fruit, then cut it down. If it bears fruit, "well and good" (Luke 13:9 NRSV).

This is a profound statement of what God's initiative in Jesus was all about. Jesus (the gardener) intervened with an impatient God (owner) and asked for time to minister to the people, one at a time. Give each person a chance to repent and to live as God's person. The kingdom of God isn't a massive war effort measurable only in gross results. The kingdom is one person called to repentance and given both time and capability for that to happen. One person, then another person, until finally creation itself sings a new song.

How you respond to God's invitation matters. Whatever your level of suffering, God isn't punishing you. God is inviting you to repent, to change your heart, to have a new mind. If you can do that, God will be merciful and forgive you. That invitation isn't some mass draft notice. It is a personal initiative just with you. And only you can accept it. Your voice in God's chorus is yours to sing.

So often, we have made submitting to the mind of God too small a thing. It can be accomplished, we say, by attending worship regularly, by volunteering at a monthly feeding ministry, or by attending a Bible study group in the neighborhood.

No, my friends, submitting to the mind of God is both huge and small. It is huge in the sense of being a total submission. It involves a turning over of one's mind, body, soul, intentionality, and actions. It is lifting up our minds to think as God thinks, to use Isaiah's language. It is passing the tests that our ancestors failed, as Paul makes clear. And it is changing our hearts and lives before it is too late, as Jesus says. That is admittedly a tall order; few attain it. But that's where the bar is set. Not a mild rearranging of one's weekly schedule, but a rethinking (repenting) of all our time. If we do less, we can ask for forgiveness and the strength to do more. But we can't preen at the small thing we did.

On the other hand, submitting to the mind of God is small in the sense that it comes down to the details and specifics of one's life. It isn't a grand gesture, but a new way of spending the next paycheck or handling the next childcare crisis or making decisions in one's career.

This raises an important question for us: What vast project of rethinking are you taking on in your own life? It's good to note smaller things, which we might call the rearranging of deck chairs. But we must also ask the serious question: What large steps am I taking? In what ways am I altering the course of the whole ship?

If your answer to that first question is "none" or "not many," ask yourself a second question: What is holding you back? What specifics are preventing you from making a necessary, large-scale change? Where are you clinging to control, rather than trusting God to show you a new path and to give you strength for submission? Make no mistake: God is calling all of us to walk this path. It's Isaiah's promise and challenge for all those who would return from exile; it's Paul's admonition for all who wish to follow Christ. And it's Christ's own invitation to repent, receive God's grace, and bear new fruit.

How will you respond to God's invitation to repentance?

GROUP STUDY GUIDE

Questions for Discussion

1. When have you experienced a difference between your plans and God's plans? How did that come about, and how did you respond to it?

2. Read Isaiah 55:1-9 again carefully. What parts of the prophet's words stands out to you the most? What is the most significant part of God's promise? What part(s) of it would you have trouble believing?

3. How do you usually conceive of God? In what ways do you see God as different from yourself, challenging you to change?

4. What connections does Paul identify between the Israelites in the wilderness and the Christians in the first century? What connections do you see between the Israelites and the Christian church today?

5. Review Paul's list of admonishments in 1 Corinthians 10:1-13. Which of these do you struggle with the most?

6. How has God given you strength to resist temptations, or "a way out" so that you can endure them?

7. We are never told the result of the parable of the fig tree in Luke 13:6-9, whether or not the tree produced fruit as a result of the gardener's efforts. Why is that? What does the open-ended story convey about God's grace and our need for repentance?

8. What do the gardener's efforts and the fertilizer represent in the parable?

9. How is Christ the gardener working in your life? What fruit does God want you to bear as a result?

Suggestions for Group Study

Learn From Past Mistakes

In 1 Corinthians 10, Paul recounts Israel's successes and failures in the wilderness (mostly failures) in order to admonish the Christians at Corinth about the way they are called to live in Christ. Read 1 Corinthians 10:1-13 as a group, making note of each time Paul refers to the Israelites in the wilderness. Then ask for volunteers to look up and read the following passages. Depending on the number of group members you have, some volunteers may need to read more than one passage or selection of passages.

Exodus 14:21-31
Exodus 16:1-36
Exodus 17:1-7; Numbers 20:1-13
Numbers 14:26-35; 26:63-65
Exodus 32:1-6
Numbers 25:1-9
Numbers 21:5-9

Discuss what lessons you as a group and/or your church might take away from these experiences. How are you tempted to grumble, to engage in immorality, to worship false gods, or to test Christ? How might you avoid these things by learning from the Israelites' example?

Turn and Bear Fruit

The root of the Greek word for repent means "to turn," so that repentance implies an act of turning, changing one's mind and behavior and starting in a new direction. If we take Jesus' call to repentance seriously, it will involve a clear change as we leave a path toward destruction and ruin and start on a path toward new life and bearing fruit for God.

Pass out index cards or small scraps of paper to each group member, and invite everyone to write down sinful behaviors or attitudes you wish to confess and repent from. Explain that these will remain confidential; members will fold their cards or pieces of paper so that no one will see what they write. Participants may write as many things as they wish. As members write what they wish to confess, ask them to bring their cards or slips of paper forward and lay them at the front of the room. You may wish to provide a table for this purpose, or simply place them on the floor.

Allow some quiet time for prayer as group members silently confess these things to God. Then as a group, turn and face the opposite direction, symbolizing that you are turning your back on these things and starting on a new path. Spend a few more moments in silence, reflecting on what new fruit God calls you each to bear as a result of your new start. If you wish, allow members to speak their responses out loud, being mindful that some participants may choose not to do so. Pray the closing prayer below as a way of asking God to grant you the strength to follow through on your act of repentance, making it a new way of life.

Closing Prayer

O God, I ache for you, and yet I know I must submit to you in order to find you. Show me the path of submission, and let me make life decisions and faith decisions that are in keeping with your desire for me. Not my will, but your will, be done. Amen.

More Than We Can Imagine

Scriptures for the
Fourth Sunday of Lent
Joshua 5:9-12
2 Corinthians 5:16-21
Luke 15:1-3, 11b-32

It's often tempting to think we have God all figured out. We know with certainty what God loathes, what God punishes, what God wants, what God rewards, and how to win God's favor. At least that's how our thinking often goes. But when we think this way, we are wrong. God is never circumscribed by our preferences or locked within the boundaries of what we can accept and understand; God is not bound by what we believe to be true. The very name God revealed to Moses means something like "I am who I am" or "I will be who I will be" (see Exodus 3:13-15). This shows what a radically open mind we should keep where God is concerned.

On my road trip, I saw one sign after another of how wretchedly whites treated Native Americans and how entire states are built on the suffering of their original inhabitants. We Americans are living a lie if any of us now think we can lecture the world on morality, as if we have an inside track on what God desires of us. Knowledge of Scripture, regular worship attendance or small group participation, prayer, or any of the other markers of Christian identity are all good things, but they don't automatically enable us to know God completely. All our Scriptures this week remind us that God is forever bigger and deeper than we can imagine.

God fed people who were ungrateful. That is so different from our human response to ingratitude. God forgave sinners and reconciled humankind. That is so different from our usual treatment of sinners. God has been like the father who showered love on a reprehensible son. That is so different from us.

These three lessons show us that we can't simply study ourselves and think we have seen the fullness of God. We do reveal something of God, and our lives are usually a good starting point for learning about God. But there is more to God than what we see in ourselves or in the things around us. Nor can we simply study the words our ancestors wrote about God. Our words and those of our forebears are inadequate to fully describe something so far beyond us. At some point, God becomes unfathomable: not just large and distant, but perplexing, behaving in ways we cannot understand or accept.

When that happens, the faithful course is to set aside what we think we know and believe to be true and to follow the strange path where God leads us. It is often the way of repentance and transformation. If we cannot let go and let God be whatever God will be, we become like the elder brother in Jesus' parable who missed the joy of his brother's return and lost connection with his father. We remain sour and bitter, unforgiving, convinced we are right. We are unable to see how far God has already moved from where we remain stuck.

THE END OF WANDERING
JOSHUA 5:9-12

The wilderness wandering didn't end with a great military victory, though there was one as Joshua led the campaign to conquer Canaan. Nor did it end with a massive show of God's power, though that happened many times too.

The wilderness wandering ended the day the Israelites "ate food produced in the land" to which God had led them (Joshua 5:11). They harvested the crops growing on the plains of Jericho, after crossing the river Jordan and leaving the wilderness behind. As they ate unleavened bread and roasted grain from the crops they gathered, it was a clear sign of transition. Now the land would support them. By eating its produce, the Israelites received God's promised gift.

On that day, the Scripture says, the manna ceased (Joshua 5:12). The bread from heaven that God had given them every morning for four decades was no longer necessary, and so it stopped. The people could now feed themselves. The manna was a hallmark of the wilderness journey, a key sign of God's ongoing providence and the people's trust in God. They gathered what they needed each day, and no more; if they tried to keep it overnight, it would spoil. The people had to trust that tomorrow's manna would come, and its daily arrival signified God's care, attention, and presence. But now the manna stopped arriving; it was never a permanent arrangement. From now on, God would provide in a different way. The land itself would be the sign of God's presence, their possession of it a sign of God's faithfulness and its produce a sign of God's favor. A new era had begun.

This new era emerged from the old. It began with circumcision and the celebration of Passover, two primary marks of the Israelites' identity and their past relationship with God (Joshua 5:1-8, 10). Circumcision was a sign of God's covenant with Abraham (see Genesis 17:9-14), and Passover was a celebration of the exodus from Egypt. As they entered the Promised Land, God cleared the way for the Israelites by rolling away an unspecified "disgrace of Egypt" (Joshua 5:9). God cleansed them, and their circumcision and Passover celebration showed that God had freed them spiritually as well as physically. God set their disgrace aside, and now so could they.

We can see in this a parallel with how God interacts with us. Many people like to believe that God has a plan for our lives. Some think that plan is quite detailed. I don't see it that way. I think God has hopes for us, not a plan.

God hopes we will move beyond our sins—that we will learn from them, seek and accept forgiveness, and not become buried in them. God hopes we will become self-sufficient, but not self-serving. God hopes we will learn to trust God, but not collapse in helplessness on God's doorstep like a child who can never grow up. God hopes we will do useful things and be generous with what we produce. God hopes we will be grateful, and not resent the times when we needed succor.

The Israelites were challenged to live in this way in the land of Canaan. The manna taught the Israelites how to trust in God and be grateful. As it stopped, they were faced with a new task: to continue relying on God even as they began to take more responsibility for their own livelihood. Now they would have to tend the land, be mindful of the year's seasons, plant and harvest crops, and eat the land's produce. Even so, they needed to remember that the land's produce was God's gift because the land itself was God's gift.

If we can learn from our wilderness experiences, here is what I think we will learn: that we are capable, that God is faithful to us, that our lives have purpose, and that we are closest to grace when we express gratitude.

Our culture tends to discourage such attitudes. We are taught to admire experts but to feel ourselves incapable. We are taught to grab what we can because the plate might not pass again. We are taught that only a few have the luxury of self-determination. We are taught to take the credit for whatever good befalls us and assign to others the blame for the bad.

Those who would follow God need to push through such cultural nonsense. It makes us small and weak, self-serving and ungrateful. We become a profit center for others and cannon fodder for their schemes when we live small in that way. On my pilgrimage Fresh Day on the Road, there came a point when I understood that this was to be a growing experience for me, a time of output. It was not a passive meandering, but a time when I would do things I had never done before. It was a time when I would produce crops—in my case, writing—that no one else could produce in exactly the same way.

Israel wasn't the only people on earth. They were probably not even the only people that God had chosen to love. God is so much larger than we tend to imagine. Like my solitary drive across country, the Israelites were a small sign of the big thing God was doing. Imagine, if you can, a world where all people feel capable, not just the dominant tribe, race, or gender. Imagine all people yearning to grow their own crops and then sharing them with others. Imagine gratitude erupting.

The wilderness wandering, you see, was ultimately about God, not just about the one tribe. The promised land of Canaan stood for all the promises that God makes to people—even to the Canaanites, whose land the Israelites took. The harvest was a sign of God's great urge to lift people out of desert places like hunger. The ceasing of the manna was a victory for God, as well as for the Israelites.

As we consider the rest of Joshua, which relates the conquest of Canaan, we might wonder whether the Israelites took from this moment a lesson that was too small. We might wonder if they saw grace flowing to their one tribe and took that to mean the ultimate superiority of their people above all others. We might wonder if they wrongfully put themselves at the center of God's creation, forgetting that God made and loved others too. We might wonder if they became

THE GIFT OF NEW CREATION

no longer a sign of God's hopes for all humankind, but the boundary of how far God would go.

Many Christians do that today in their disregard for the suffering of many people. As long as the Christian enterprise is victorious, we believe, it matters little if people are hurt along the way. It feels good to be part of the chosen tribe, but it makes God too small.

How can you be a sign of God's hope for all of humankind?

THE MINISTRY OF RECONCILIATION
2 CORINTHIANS 5:16-21

On US 550 from Farmington, New Mexico, to Albuquerque, I had a brief experience that was disturbing and yet uplifting.

The Navajo Nation was behind me, and my route took me by the Jicarilla Apache Reservation and the Jemez Pueblo. It was unpromising land with few signs of development other than oil rigs. I saw a sign for Zia Pueblo and decided to drive into it and look around. I immediately ran into signs saying, "No cameras. No sketches. No sound recorders. No video." As I continued driving, I saw more and more of these signs.

The message was clear: "Leave us alone. We aren't here for your entertainment." I was initially disturbed by the words and the sentiment behind them. I had thought myself a sympathetic friend, not a tourist who had come to feed on their poverty. But I had to admit that, to their eyes, I was just a tourist. I was an outsider, and to take a photograph or recording would have been to use their identity and reality for my purposes, not theirs. I respected their wishes, left my iPhone camera in my car's cup holder, and drove away quickly.

As I drove on, I thought to myself, "Good for them." It was bad enough to have their ancestral lands taken by whites. Why should they now be entertainment for descendants of those whites? Why should their culture be something for others to study, admire, or discuss? Why should their likeness serve the purposes of outsiders? I applauded their assertiveness.

For this impasse to end, we need to become what Paul called "new creation" (2 Corinthians 5:17). We can't rewrite the Native Americans' tragic history. But we can find new ground and be reconciled. I have no idea how that can occur. But I know, by faith, that it is a possibility.

Being reconciled is far more than simply becoming friends. It means stepping away from positions long held, attitudes long practiced, grievances long felt, and finding new ground entirely. It happens when all parties commit themselves to focus on their shared future rather than a tragic past—not because the past doesn't matter, but because a future together matters more. Reconciliation happens when enmity ends, not because everyone feels happier but because enemies have chosen to stop hating. It happens when people who have significant issues with each other decide there is something more important than pursuing those issues.

Reconciliation stands at the heart of Paul's words in 2 Corinthians 5:16-21. The God who sends new things has "reconciled us to himself through Christ." This same God has given to Paul and his compatriots the "ministry of reconciliation" (5:18). And as representatives of Christ, Paul implores the Corinthian church to "be reconciled to God" (5:20). This is the message of reconciliation that Paul carries: Through Christ, God has reconciled the world to himself by no longer counting people's sins against them. God has opened a way of reconciliation, and the people of the world are called to receive this gift of God's grace.

Paul understood that God had longstanding, legitimate, and corrosive issues with humanity. People had sinned against one another, they had taken the life of God's Son, and they had violated God's clear desires. That was the story of humankind in general and God's chosen people, Israel specifically. It was a tragic past, which amounted to a repeated rejection of God and violence, exploitation, and injustice toward one another.

But God had chosen to reconcile the world to God, to let the "old things" go away so that new things could arrive (2 Corinthians 5:17). God would no longer be at odds with humanity, not even with those who violated Jesus. Rather, in Christ, God wrote a new chapter. God "reconciled us [Paul and his fellow believers] to himself through Christ" (5:18). Then God gave that "ministry of reconciliation" to these Christian "ambassadors" (5:20). Through them, God was reconciling the world to himself. And this is nothing less than a "new creation" for those who are in Christ (5:17).

Central to reconciliation is the ability to see other people in a new way. "From this point on we won't recognize people by human standards," Paul said, for that point of view leads to enmity (2 Corinthians 5:16). Christ, through whom reconciliation comes, must be known in a new way, not by human standards (5:16). By human standards, Christ was nothing more than a troublemaker who was crucified. If we see in this way, the effects of the tragic past continue. But, Paul says, we must know Christ in another way, as he really is: one whose death was for the sake of all, and who was raised from the dead (5:15). Only by seeing Christ in this way can we see the path to reconciliation. Then comes a decision to "be reconciled," that we might "become the righteousness of God" (5:20-21).

As ambassadors of Christ, we are called to pursue reconciliation with one another as a sign of God's reconciliation of the world. That is how we carry out the ministry and message of reconciliation. Christians are to be peacemakers, not advocates for division, even division grounded in perceived right-opinion. Christians are to build bridges over the chasms, heal the broken, and think themselves no better than others. Jesus "became sin," that is, became human and God's offering, so that we could see what true humanity looks like when the old is set aside and new creation is allowed to happen.

How can you be a messenger of reconciliation?

THE GREAT SCANDAL
LUKE 15:1-3, 11b-32

The great scandal of our faith is that God is merciful. God is more aptly compared to a forgiving parent than a hard-minded judge. Our God doesn't keep score, smite the lowly, or reject sinners.

All the cruel and judgmental attitudes that are often ascribed to God are simply wrong. They are a projection of ourselves onto God. We reject this group or that group. We call them sinners. We say God loathes them. We claim to be doing God's work when we oppress them. These mindsets may be what we hold to be true, but they are not a true reflection of God.

Jesus scandalized the religious people of his age by welcoming sinners and eating with them. They muttered against him, so he told a parable—which we know as the parable of the prodigal son—about a son who went far astray and turned against his father (Luke 15:11-32). When the son came to his senses, he realized that he'd be better off as a servant in his father's house than in the foreign land where he was living. Thinking he could not possibly return to the status of "son" after leaving his family behind and squandering his inheritance, he determined to return in the role of a slave. The father nevertheless welcomed him home as a son, with open arms and a great banquet. But the son's older brother son hated this welcome reception of the son who had gone away (Luke 15:25-32). He resented his father's kindness toward one who had shown he didn't deserve it.

Christians throughout the years have decided Jesus was wrong in this parable. To be sure, we haven't come out and said that outright. But we do usually ignore the parable and go about our preferred work of rejecting sinners, treating them as outcasts, even assaulting and killing them. How many of us truly side with the father in this parable in the way we behave? If we're honest, we must admit that the older brother bears more of a resemblance to us. While most Christians know this parable, few actually intend to follow its teaching.

How could God be so unlike us? I think that is the starting point for addressing this parable, indeed for addressing faith in general. As Isaiah said in last week's Old Testament reading, God's ways are not our ways, and our ways are not God's ways (Isaiah 55:8-9). It isn't so much that God is more powerful than us, sometimes in ways that seem magical, but that God is merciful, kind, forgiving, and accepting. We think our intolerance is a virtue, but all it does is show how little we understand of God.

God loves all that God has made. That love, not an ancient or modern moral code, is our foundation. When Jesus looked at a woman caught in adultery, he saw a child of God rather than an enemy of the religious order. The same was true when he saw a prostitute, or a rich man willing to hurt others to protect his wealth, or a Gentile, or a Roman soldier, or a fool like Simon. Jesus welcomed them all, for they were all children of God.

It is difficult to imagine worse sins than those the prodigal son committed. He turned against his father by asking for his inheritance.

As the younger of two sons, he would inherit a third of his father's estate, with his older brother receiving two-thirds (see Deuteronomy 21:17). But by asking for the inheritance before his father died, he showed that he cared more for the property than the relationship with his family. In effect, he turned his back on his family in order to live life his own way. But, of course, he wanted to do so with his share of the family's wealth.

Not only did the son leave his family behind, but he "took a trip to a land far away" (Luke 15:13). The CEB Study Bible suggests that in order to do so, the young son may have sold his property rights to another person, turning the property into liquid wealth (*The CEB Study Bible with Apocrypha*, New Testament page 144). Doing so would have diminished his family's land holdings. While in this far-away land, he wasted his inheritance—his father's wealth—through dissolute living. After his money ran out, he hired himself out feeding pigs. This represents rock bottom for the young man. Pigs were considered unclean animals, and a righteous Jew would have avoided them. He separated himself from his Jewish heritage as well as from his family.

And yet, when the prodigal son came to his senses and returned to his father, his father ran to greet him. The father ignored his son's willingness to serve as a slave. He treated him as a member of the household. When the elder son bitterly rejected such mercy, the father said the son's return mattered more than any human calculations of what is fitting. It was as though his son had died and come back to life.

This story was an over-the-top response to some muttering about Jesus welcoming sinners to his presence and eating with them. But that is the nature of God: over-the-top, loving in ways we cannot imagine loving, forgiving those whom we cannot imagine forgiving, feeling a gladness that we don't share, showing a magnanimity that we don't allow. It is a great scandal . . . unless we too can love as God loves.

Imagine what it's like to be on the receiving end of such love. We thought we were lost and despised, and here is God embracing us. We thought we deserved the opprobrium of the righteous, and here is God ignoring our failings out of the sheer joy of seeing us return. Jesus upended everything the religious leaders believed to be true. And whenever Christians behave like the super-pious and smug people who turned against Jesus, we show our need to hear this parable again and again.

If we set our minds on true repentance, I think we must face up to two realities. The first is that the God we think we know is, in all likelihood, a compendium of preferences, attitudes, and prejudices that spring from within us rather than from God's self-revelation. The endless bickering over women's freedom or homosexuals' rights, for example, has virtually nothing to do with God's self-revelation. Merely quoting Leviticus 18:22 adds nothing, especially when we ignore much else in Leviticus because we deem it irrelevant to our times. Baptizing our personal preferences and wrapping them in Scripture is a poor substitute for ethical inquiry, not to mention biblical scholarship.

The second reality we must face is the consequence of the first. When we project our preferences, attitudes, and prejudices onto God, we manipulate God into condoning, even requiring, the enslavement of peoples, the land grabs common in conquest, and the treatment of enemies and minorities as subhuman. If we truly repent, we must acknowledge that we cast God in our own image and, in doing so, we drag God down into our sin.

It isn't enough to say, "Well, I think slavery is wrong, and I have found a few Bible passages that affirm my view." And we surely must not conclude, as a Bible-thumping preacher in Arizona recently said, "Well, I think homosexuals deserve to be executed, and here are verses and church teachings that show I am right." Neither side of our cultural divides has truly engaged the mind and heart of God. For God is so much more than we can imagine. Repentance involves acknowledging that the articles of our religion have too much to do with us.

The question for you, therefore, is twofold: Are you prepared to set aside what you think you know about God and to let God be God? And, can you imagine God relating to you in languages and categories beyond what you prefer?

Neither question points to an easy answer. Repentance is never easy. Both will require more silence before God and more humility. Are you ready to be silent and humble?

What attitudes about God do you need to set aside in repentance?

GROUP STUDY GUIDE

Questions for Discussion

1. Have you ever been surprised by God? What was it about this experience that surprised you?

2. How do you respond to a revelation that you didn't see coming?

3. What have you learned from wilderness experiences about yourself or God? How did these experiences transform you so that you lived or thought differently afterwards?

4. Have you ever found yourself stuck in a stereotype that had been imposed by someone else? What did you do to assert yourself and your real nature? How did people respond to you?

5. Can you think of a moment when you chose to see someone else in a new way? What was the result of this decision?

6. Have you ever deliberately set out to reconcile with someone with whom you had differences? Or, have you ever been the recipient of someone's efforts to reconcile? What was that experience like?

7. How has your relationship with God changed and matured over time? What attitudes or practices have you let go of or taken on in order to know God in a new way?

8. When have you felt the extravagance of God's grace at work in your life?

9. When have you embodied God's extravagant grace to another person? Or how can you do that in the near future?

Suggestions for Group Study

Exploring Our Ideas of God

When it comes to talking about God, we very quickly push up against the limitations of our own language and ability to think. As a group, brainstorm all the words, concepts, and images you use to talk about God. Write these down on a markerboard, chalkboard, large piece of paper, or some other surface. Try to generate a list that is as large and diverse as possible. Spend a few minutes reflecting on your list out loud together, making note especially of things that surprise you and things that seem to represent God for a large portion of your group.

Next, play a short game in which volunteers will attempt to draw a picture using as many of the words or concepts that your group has listed. Here is how it will work:

Two volunteers will each have two minutes to draw a single picture that encompasses as many of the words, concepts, or images that you have listed as possible. At the end of the two minutes, each volunteer will have thirty seconds to explain his or her picture and which of the words or concepts it attempted to illustrate. The remaining group members will vote on whose picture best captured the list you generated. *Note that the volunteers are not trying to draw a picture of God; they are trying to create a single picture that best illustrates the breadth of imagery that your group associates with God.

Repeat this exercise with two more volunteers, and continue for as long as your group prefers. Then discuss the following questions:

Why is it so hard to capture our ideas of God in a single image?

Who provided the best representation of our full list? Why?

What did you discover about our ways of understanding God through this exercise?

Review our images and your list of words or concepts one more time. What aspects of God have we left out? Conclude with a moment of quiet prayer together, asking God for grace to see God more clearly and fully, recognizing that God will always be beyond our complete understanding.

Enact the Parable of the Prodigal Son

Entering into the biblical story can help us identify with the perspectives of the characters. In this activity, group members will adopt the perspective of the prodigal son, the father, or the older brother by writing a short letter or giving a brief speech from his perspective.

Assign each group member one of the three roles in the parable of the prodigal son: the son, the father, or the brother. Give each member a piece of paper and a pen or pencil, and ask them to write a letter from the perspective of their assigned character. The letter should be addressed to the other two characters. So the prodigal son will write to his father and his brother; the brother will write to his father and the son; and the father will write to his two sons. Use the biblical story in Luke 15 as a starting point, but be creative in imagining your character's emotions, motivations, and thought patterns. If time permits, invite one or more group members to share their letters with the rest of the group.

As an alternative, members can prepare and deliver a short speech to the whole group describing the characters' emotions and motivations that drove their actions. The idea should be to explain to outsiders why they behaved as they did in the story. After letters have been written or speeches delivered, conclude this exercise by discussing the following questions:

What did you learn by embodying the perspective of your character?

Which character in the story do you sympathize with the most? Why?

How does this story challenge your notion of God? How did this exercise help you to see this parable in a new light?

How can you use the insights of this story, or of this exercise, to help you live out the "ministry of reconciliation" that God calls us to?

Closing Prayer

O God, take the blinders from my eyes, the stops from my ears, and the hardness from my heart. Help me to do what you want me to do, not what I want to do. Help me to go where you want me to go, not where I want to go. May I be humble in a world of hubris, gentle in a world of cruelty, and quiet in a world of noise. Amen.

A New Thing

Scriptures for the
Fifth Sunday of Lent
Isaiah 43:16-21
Philippians 3:4b-14
John 12:1-8

This week's lessons are about the "new things" God is doing. In a sense, they capture the entire sweep of the Old and New Testaments.

As the Old Testament makes clear, God moves on from "prior things," forgives past sins, calls people to new life, and then helps to make it happen. We might cling to old ways, from old habits to old traditions to old religion based on old words, but God moves forward. The former things become a foretaste and a guarantee of the new things God will do. How else could the Israelites in exile believe Isaiah's promise that new life awaited them in Zion?

Paul saw his own life as proof of that restless newness that God brings about. He saw his former self lost in the virtues and sins of an old way of living. But by the grace of the risen Christ who came to him, God moved him forward to new life. He wasn't there yet, but he pressed on to the goal set for him by God.

Another small example of the new things God brings about was the incident at the home of Lazarus in Bethany. There Mary behaved in a totally new way, anointing Jesus with costly perfume. It was shocking. But Jesus said she was right to do it. This anointing honored the new thing that he was about to do and the new relationship that would exist for all of them when that new thing was accomplished.

The tensions in faith communities, like the tensions in society, often exist between former things and new things. The custodians of former things tend to be a powerful constituency. The new things often begin among the less powerful. That's why change is so often slow and why rapid change is often painful and chaotic. The old order doesn't give ground without a fight.

Faith communities should be attentive to radical newness, because that is so often where God is active. In fact, however, religion usually allies itself with old orders. This week's lessons urge the faithful to repent of clinging to old ways and to embrace, with excitement and gratitude, the new things God is doing. When we do, we will find that the "prior things" have not been abandoned but fulfilled, taken up in the larger story God is writing.

LETTING GO OF THE PAST
ISAIAH 43:16-21

On my 4,100-mile pilgrimage by car, I was never far from history with all of its warts. I started in northern California: a mecca of new technology, yet already being stained by neo-Gilded Age greed and crass displays of wealth.

In the Mojave Desert, I could see the ghosts of dust bowl Okies desperately heading west in search of work. I could also see their latter-day successors, Mexican immigrants fleeing poverty. It reminded me that history repeats itself.

In Arizona, New Mexico, and Oklahoma, I came across the stories of native tribes forced onto barren reservations far from their homes so that whites could claim their more promising lands in the southeast and the southwest.

I listened on my car radio to a drumbeat of white resentment aimed at people of color. It was as if the Civil War had just ended, and the fact that the president at the time was black was just one more assault on white superiority. I hadn't known how much anger and fear are out there.

I also ran across better signs: tolerance at ground level, diversity assumed and respected, people putting history behind them. But I never stopped hearing rage and dismay stoked by memories.

I am mindful of Mississippi writer William Faulkner's observation that Southerners have trouble letting go of the past. I don't think it's just Southerners, though. Faulker's comment that "the past isn't even past" applies to many people, from spouses trapped in the rancor of "you always" and "you never" to victims of abuse to people laid off from work to minorities targeted for bullying.

THE GIFT OF NEW CREATION

Religion, unfortunately, often reinforces the lifeless burden of history. It shouldn't surprise us: Our Scriptures, after all, are revered ancient texts. It's a way of keeping the sacred past alive in our memories. But it can also be a way of killing a fresh faith in the present. Too often, laws first written for Bronze Age nomads are kept alive as moral codes for the twenty-first century. Homosexual persons find themselves hated because of Leviticus 18:22. Women can't escape the patriarchal patterns that governed life in ancient Palestine. The burdens just keep piling on, and the past becomes a dead weight that holds us back instead of an energy that pushes us forward.

For the people of Judah, the past had become just such a burden. Isaiah—or more properly Second Isaiah, the author of Isaiah 40–55—wrote to the people of Judah who were in exile in Babylon. For these people, the distant past still contained its high points, prosperous years, and events worthy of celebration: a covenant with the ancestors, the exodus from Egypt, the laws given at Sinai, the wilderness wandering, the possession of the land, and the golden age of king David. But the recent past had cast their history in a new, negative light. The people of Judah had broken the covenant God made with their ancestors. Once again they found themselves held captive by a foreign people. They had lost the land. Kings had become weak and unrighteous. David's everlasting kingdom had fallen, and so had the Temple, the sign of God's presence and favor. The people in exile bore the weight of their ancestor's failures. What good was the distant past for them? It symbolized only a burden that their more recent forebears had proven themselves unable to carry.

Imagine yourself living in exile in Babylon under these circumstances. One day, a prophet comes to you and invites you to go home to your ancestral land. Why should you go? A fearsome desert lies in the way, and you don't know the way across. Moreover, as far as you are concerned there is no life there. Your sins and the sins of your ancestors still lie heavy on your back.

Isaiah spoke a breathtaking word to the Israelites, a word so fresh and radical that even today many of us are tempted to ignore it.

Isaiah said that God would tame the desert. The first words of today's passage are a clear echo of the exodus story, when God brought the Israelites out of Egypt. Isaiah reminds his audience that the LORD who speaks to them is the one who "makes a way in the sea, and a path in the mighty waters" (Isaiah 43:16). This God "brings out chariot and horse, army and battalion," luring Pharaoh and his army into a spectacular defeat at the Sea of Reeds in which "they will be extinguished, extinguished like a wick" (43:17). Now, Isaiah promises, God will do it again—not a repetition, but a "new thing" that will be just as wonderful and foundational for their life going forward. Just as God made a dry path through the sea, God will now make a well-watered way through the desert (43:19-20). Earlier in Isaiah 43, God gives a simple reason why: "Because you are precious in my eyes, you are honored, and I love you" (43:4).

Then the prophet said, "Don't remember the prior things; don't ponder ancient history" (Isaiah 43:18). This is a radical command for a people admonished time and again to remember the past, lest their identity be forgotten. Instead, the people are urged to pay attention to God's "new thing" (43:19). History had become a weight, and now God gave them the opportunity to turn the page and begin again. If God's unconditional love is the foundation of their hope, this lifting of history's burden is their sustenance.

"Look! I'm doing a new thing; now it sprouts up; don't you recognize it?" (Isaiah 43:19). To a people steeped in history but now buried in history, never able to rise beyond ancient failings and to breathe the free air of new life, the prophet proclaimed a "new thing." It is enough to make even wild animals honor God, and the arid wilderness to yield water (43:20).

Jesus proclaimed a new thing centuries later, when he saw God doing a novel thing in him and setting humanity free from its history.

The keepers of that history never want to hear about new things. New things are a threat, something to be feared, and so we fall back on our old stories even when they become burdensome. We must be wary of building our enterprises solely on undying memories and old words treated as burning embers. We must resist the impulse to treat everything God has ever said and done as totally alive and normative today. Whenever we live completely in the past, we live as opponents of the prophet's hopeful message. Isaiah clearly said that "prior things" were to be forgotten and "new things" welcomed.

Might it be that people turn away from Christianity when they find within it an unyielding—and self-serving—imposition of old things? What if they saw instead evidence of God doing something new in our hearts and lives?

God wants life, not death. God wants praise, not compulsory obedience. God wants freedom, not fear. Many Christians have built franchises on the reverence, almost worship, of ancient words and keeping old things alive. It's time we all left that exile and followed a God of new things to whatever land God would show us next. Whatever we think we know, God wants to show us new things.

What new thing is God trying to show you? What prior thing does God want you to forget?

FALSE GODS AND THE TRUE GOD
PHILIPPIANS 3:4b-14

In my work with people caught in addiction, I heard echoes of Paul all the time. "I had it all," they would say. They boasted of a good job, a loving family, good health, a house, a car, and other blessings. Then, one asset at a time, they lost it. As their drinking or drug use spiraled out of control, they alienated their family, sacrificed their health, and, usually last, lost their jobs.

In faith terms, they gave their lives to the wrong god. That god betrayed them. Nothing got better until they came to believe there was a true God (or Higher Power, to use the language of twelve-step programs) who could restore their lives to sanity. Things improved as they sought through prayer and meditation to grow in conscious contact with that God. It's a pattern of being lost, and then being found.

This phenomenon of being lost and then found applies to people other than addicts. Any time we give ourselves to a false god, we lose our way. It might be a career, material success, money, physical appearance, sex, or popularity; that false god has many faces in today's world. The lure tends to be what Satan promised Jesus in the wilderness: Give your loyalty to me, and I will give you great power, wealth, and worldly respect.

Though Paul doesn't use this exact language, it's clear that he had worshiped a false god earlier in his life. He never would have admitted as much; he prided himself on being a faithful Jew, and in his way of life eschewing false gods was quite literally rule number one. But Paul did have a false god, namely "confidence in physical advantages" (Philippians 3:4). Though in his mind he worshiped the true God, Paul eventually came to understand that he had worshiped his religion instead. He was a fervent practitioner of religion, indeed a "soldier" defending his religion, but he did not know anything beyond the flesh.

Paul had every reason to boast in his "physical advantages," which he lists in Philippians 3:5-6. He had been circumcised on the eighth day, according to Jewish custom. He was an Israelite, a member of the prominent tribe of Benjamin, a true Hebrew of the Hebrews. He was a Pharisee, devoted to the proper observation of the Law, and had even gone so far as to harass the Christians because of his zeal for his religion. He could rightly call himself "blameless" as far as the Law was concerned. The point he seems to make is this: If anybody is to benefit from devoting himself to such a god as "physical advantages," it is Paul. Nobody could possibly do it better.

Then he met Christ Jesus, and everything changed. Paul came to face with the true God, revealed in Jesus. In giving his life to Jesus, he lost all that he had before. But he counted that loss as "sewer trash," because he came to know that they had never been worthy of his wholehearted devotion. He discovered, instead, the "superior value of knowing Christ Jesus my Lord" (Philippians 3:8).

Paul came to know a faith that went deeper than righteousness in the Law. He knew the power of Jesus' resurrection. He came to believe that he should share in the sufferings of Jesus and thus become "conformed to his death," so that he might also be made like Christ in his resurrection (Philippians 3:10).

Though not a humble man by nature, Paul saw that he had far to go before he could fully share in the life, death, and resurrection of Jesus. It's not a goal that he believed he had reached. He forgot what lay behind him and reached out for the things ahead (Philippians 3:13), pursuing "the prize of God's upward call in Christ Jesus" (3:14).

It's ironic that Paul recounts his past life and then a few sentences later says, "I forget about the things behind me" (Philippians 3:13). Paul didn't adopt amnesia. It was important to him that he remember his former days, but he had to put them aside. They no longer defined him. If he attained any righteousness, it wouldn't be the formulaic uprightness of solid religion. By faith he would come to share in the righteousness of Jesus.

THE GIFT OF NEW CREATION

Losing our way is part of the human condition. To some extent, it is inevitable that our health will peak and then fade, our relationships will dwindle to a few, and our resources will be stretched thin. That's the way life goes. It's also probable that we will make wrong choices, often chasing false gods as our ancestors in faith did time and time again. Some of us will lose naturally, and others of us will lose through wrong choices. And still others will, like Paul, lose seemingly everything by making a right choice, choosing to follow Christ even when it will cost us much.

However we lose—whether by the normal passing of time, the making of wrong choices, or the decision to follow Jesus—we face the same dilemma Paul faced: Did we lose anything that matters, and should we therefore be filled with regret? Or is the loss of all things insignificant compared to the joy of knowing God through Jesus and in the power of the Spirit?

Paul concluded that his losses didn't matter, because he had found something of far greater value, namely, "God's upward call in Christ Jesus."

How is God calling you upward?

EYES TO SEE AND COURAGE TO LOOK
JOHN 12:1-8

When I returned home from my 4,100-mile pilgrimage across the United States, I parked my car in the driveway and hoped never to sit in it again. That was unrealistic, of course, but it was a sign of my struggle to get off the road and back into my regular life. It took me three days of feeling flat and uninspired before I felt normal again.

That struggle was an important time. It wasn't just something to be endured. I could learn from it. I could see God in it. In a blog post, I wrote that I was "home, but not home." That sense of already, but not yet resonated with many of my online readers. My three days of uncertainty also made the fourth day richer. It was a Sunday, and I ventured into a new church where I had a wonderful experience. I know my experience there stemmed partly from the three days of struggle that preceded it.

Our journey with God is always changing. It never follows a script. But there is one thing I notice time and again: If I look deeply, I can see God in each moment. Even, or maybe especially, in the difficult ones. I just have to look and not be satisfied with a superficial glance.

The dinner in Bethany was this kind of a moment for the friends of Jesus. They could take it as just a meal. Or they could follow Mary's lead and look deeply at what was happening. The author of the Fourth Gospel doesn't explain how Mary came to her understanding. Somehow she had grasped that Jesus was entering his final days. The religious establishment would soon rise up against him to protect their interests. Anticipating his death and burial, she performed a ritual that not only showed respect for him as a living person but laid the ground for anointing his body after death.

One of the disciples, Judas Iscariot, saw only the superficial: He was missing an opportunity to steal some money from the common purse. He tried to mask his crass worry in a concern for the poor. But the author of John's Gospel wasn't fooled. We are not told, but it's easy to imagine the other disciples had more genuine reactions against Mary's behavior. Perhaps Peter or John did wonder how many poor people could benefit from the proceeds of such expensive perfume. Martha or Lazarus may have been embarrassed by the actions of their sister. Maybe some of the diners were unsettled, or simply annoyed by this interruption of their meal. It was a moment they likely considered with a glance and then hoped to move on as quickly as possible. I wonder how many of them looked long enough to see God within it?

Jesus, on the other hand, affirmed Mary's lavish anointing of him with costly perfume. As he saw it, her act prepared the way for burial rituals, and it showed respect for him as a friend about to leave their company. I hear mockery in his comment to Judas about always having the poor with them: Judas can steal from the purse another day. Jesus' death and burial are drawing near, and only Mary recognizes it. Mary is the one who saw rightly, and Jesus helped the disciples—and us—to see as she did.

The meaning for us, it seems to me, is to keep on looking deeply even at the most wearisome moments. We can see God's presence in everything, but only if we look below the surface. Jesus wasn't just a buddy over for yet another meal. He was their rabbi, he was facing stiff opposition, he was preparing himself for suffering and death, and he was spending this preparation time with them. He was allowing them to come into the moment with him.

One aspect of faith is the desire, and ability, to live in the moment but also to live inside the moment. It's the ability to go about normal things, but at the same time to walk deeply into the meaning of things. It's to be with familiar people, but also to experience their deeper side. It's to be eating a meal, in this case, but also to sense the much deeper drama taking place around it.

Faith gives us eyes to see such things, and faith gives us the courage to look. We don't stay on the surface, where safety prevails. We go deeper because that is where meaning lies.

As I drew near the Mississippi River on my journey, I imagined a pivotal event: crossing from West to East, from the land settlers crossed and claimed to the older regions where they were too poor to remain or too restless. I would pass from a land that had been divided by civil strife to a land that had been torn apart, decimated, bloodied—a land filled with graves and monuments and simmering resentments. I know my American history and geography, and I expected this crossing to have *meaning*.

The river always wins, however. It overflows its banks every spring and sends silt-filled water flooding onto farmlands. Houses and barns are built on high perches that the water usually won't reach. The highway starts up an incline at least ten miles from the river, maybe twenty. I lost track of where I was. The ascending road just went on and on, and my surroundings became wetter and wetter. I kept looking for that one vista that would show the river itself. Instead, I just saw water spreading far and wide, and I knew that, somewhere in the middle, there was a deeper channel where my ancestors raced riverboats in the 1850s.

On the other side, Tennessee looked the same as the land I had left behind. It was more like a continuation of Arkansas than a break from the West. Similar stories were also told about western Tennessee: rooting out native tribes so that whites could have their land and homes, Civil War battles, and forts that served moneyed interests. For an evening, I literally had no idea where I was.

The issue, of course, was expectations. This is the same issue we face constantly in faith. I expected reality to be a certain way, just as I have expected God to be a certain way. My expected scenario might be different from yours. We might well argue about whose scenario is correct. The fact is, however, that the river always wins.

God always wins; we can no more fence God in than we can control the river's mighty flow. God will show us what God wants to show us, where it pleases God, when it pleases God, and with outcomes that God desires.

When we seek God, we had better be prepared to come to a river that is beyond our control. Can you do that? Leave aside your sense of biblical prowess and your years of being steeped in religious tradition. Can you come to the river today and deal with a flood you didn't ask for and a sense of time and place that don't obey your scripts? Can you let yourself feel lost? Or will you be so desperate not to be lost and not to be out of control that you pretend to see vistas your mind created, rather than the vistas that God, in all reality, is showing you?

How do your expectations need to change today? What moments do you need to see with new eyes?

GROUP STUDY GUIDE

Questions for Discussion

1. Where do you see the tension between old ways and new ways in your life? in your church? in your community? in the world around us?

2. To what extent is your faith grounded in old traditions and habits, and to what extent is it open to new, even surprising experiences? How do you maintain a balance between these two aspects of faith?

3. What old things did the Israelites in exile need to leave behind in order to come home? What new thing was God calling them to as a result?

4. What false gods are you tempted to put before the one true God?

5. What have you given up, or lost, for the sake of Christ? What is your attitude toward that loss?

6. What might God be calling you to give up now, for the first time, in order to follow Christ more faithfully?

7. Can you identify a moment in the last year like the dinner at Bethany, when you became aware of something deeper than what was happening on the surface? What did it take for you to see God in that moment?

8. What new thing has God shown you lately? How were you surprised by it, and how did you respond to it?

Suggestions for Group Study

Faith Family Tree

In Philippians 3, Paul makes much of his impressive faith pedigree only to tear down its edifice in order to point to Christ. As we read about his background, we can see how deeply Paul's faith was formed by his past and his religious heritage. All of us are, like Paul, formed in faith by those who have gone before us.

Give everyone a sheet of paper and a pen or pencil, and explain to group members that you will each attempt to trace your "faith pedigree" like Paul did in Philippians, in order to explore the factors that have influenced your faith most deeply. Instruct each participant to list the three people who have influenced his or her faith the most, along with a brief description of why they were so influential. The influence need not be entirely positive. Answers may include parents, a pastor, a youth worker, a friend, a coworker, or any other individual.

Next, ask participants to consider each of the individuals they have named, and identify the three biggest faith influences in each of their lives. Answers may include other individuals (parent, mentor, and so forth), but may also be something else such as the Bible, The United Methodist Church, a weekly church group, or a significant experience or event. For any individuals that are named in this second step, repeat the exercise a third time, continuing back as far as you can.

Hopefully, each person will recognize at least one or two aspects of his or her faith that have been passed down. Even those who are relatively new to the Christian faith should be able to name a person who has taught and mentored them. Spend some time allowing participants to share their faith family trees with one another; then discuss the following questions:

What is the most well-established influence on your faith, according to the family tree you just made?

Were there any negative aspects of your faith that you identified? How might you respond to these in your current practice of faith?

What new thing is God doing in your life that might surprise some of the individuals you have named?

How can you be a significant influence on someone else? What are you passing on to your friends, your coworkers, your children, or others in your circle of relationships?

The Prior Things

Isaiah makes a mention of "the prior things" and "ancient history," an implied reference to God's mighty acts in the past such as the exodus from Egypt (Isaiah 43:16-18). Scripture has several summaries of God's past acts on Israel's behalf, what we might call a "historical recap" that allows the people to commemorate the ways God has come to their rescue. One striking example is Joshua 24:1-13, which sets the stage for a renewal of the covenant after the Israelites have taken possession of the Promised Land.

As a group, read Joshua 24:1-13 out loud. Then take a few moments to consider what you might add to Joshua's narrative based on what God did after the conquest of Canaan. What are the important milestones in the history of the Christian faith?

List these milestones on a markerboard, chalkboard, or large sheet of paper, placing events into one of three categories: biblical events; events in church history; and modern events in the recent past. Examples might include David and Goliath; the Last Supper; the Crusades; and the Civil Rights Movement. Identify how God has acted in each of these events and what these events say about God's relationship with God's people and humankind in general.

Now ask: What new things might we expect from God in the near future? Make a fourth list of how you might expect God to show up in your community or in our world at large. Conclude with a few moments of quiet prayer, asking for eyes to see the new thing that God is doing today.

Closing Prayer

O God, show me your new things for creation. And when my heart is ready, show me your new things for me. Help me to accept not knowing where I am, so that you can show me. Help me to see beyond my control to that new vista you are eager to show me. Amen.

The Search for Meaning

Isaiah 50:4-9a
Philippians 2:5-11
Luke 22:14–23:56

Early Christians told many stories about Jesus. Some they knew in common, and some were unique to a particular congregation. The point of the storytelling wasn't to formulate a biography of the man or an exact history of his life. The people were searching for meaning. What had been the meaning of Jesus' life, death, and resurrection? What was their purpose now as Jesus people? What new thing was God doing?

In time, beginning around 70 A.D. or more than thirty years after Jesus died, unknown authors sorted through these stories. Using a new literary form called *Gospel*, these authors presented the stories of Jesus' life, death, and resurrection in ways that conveyed what it all meant. It's been said that the Gospels can be understood as passion narratives with extended introductions—meaning that the Gospel writers spent a great deal of time and attention on the suffering and death of Jesus. In a way, it's as if they each presented a Passion narrative, with enough material attached to it to explain what the Passion meant.

Again, the Gospels are not understood best as history or biography, but as quests for meaning. We need to read these Gospels in a way that honors their goal: as guides to meaning in our own lives.

Many of us are tempted to take these four Gospels literally, indeed to take the entirety of Scripture literally, as if every story, every choice of word, flowed from the mind of God. That sounds good, and it has enabled a class of Bible scholars and preachers to claim all truth. Meaning, however, doesn't arise from ascribing divine magic to human words. It comes when we grapple with how earlier people understood what they believed, and how today's people grapple with God's presence in their lives. That is the way of ambiguity, uncertainty, mystery, and humility, and many simply don't like it.

This week's three lessons include Isaiah's grappling with human suffering and Paul's grappling with the ironies that surrounded Jesus. But the centerpiece is the Passion in the Gospel according to Luke. This is Luke's take on what happened to Jesus and what it meant. Similar, though not identical, stories are told by the other three evangelists.

I haven't tried to reduce Luke's Passion Gospel to a few pithy summary statements. Instead, I have tried to understand each stage in the journey from Last Supper to Golgotha. As you grapple with the lessons, wrestle in your own way with the meaning of Christ's suffering in your life.

THE SUFFERING SERVANT
ISAIAH 50:4-9a

When people suffer, they often ask, "Did I deserve that?" They think deserving it has something to do with suffering. Some, maybe even many of us, think that suffering comes as a punishment for sin. Some who suffer think it's because they offended God.

It's comforting, in a way, to blame myself for suffering or to blame some power that is out to get me. The idea that suffering is largely random, a function mostly of chance, and too much to bear. Who could live in such a random universe? How do I avoid suffering if I can't name cause and effect when it occurs and then vow to avoid those causes from now on? What's the point of repentance if it doesn't get me something in return, namely, exemption from further suffering-as-punishment?

We want order in our world. We want reasons. In other words, we want control. If nothing else, we want God to be in control. Wrong place at the wrong time? Not good enough. Bad luck? Not good enough. The one case in ten thousand that leads to death? Not good enough. We want cause and effect. We want answers. It amazes me how we are often willing to turn God into a monster in order to prove cause and effect. We blame God for "closing doors," for "wanting Mom to come home," for enforcing some iron law of spiritual consequences, or for not "listening" to my prayers because I am unworthy. We say God killed sinners, that God killed David's son to punish David's sin of adultery, or that God killed Jesus in order to wipe humankind's slate clean.

The problem comes, of course, when we look at truly undeserved suffering—like a child dying of starvation in Honduras or a girl abused by her father. In the face of this, we can do little more than analyze causes and punish perpetrators, but the undeserved suffering remains. Our search for causes and effects ends up paralyzing us.

This very question has tormented believers back to the beginning of belief. It's one reason the ancients told the story of Adam and Eve and blamed their sin and resulting punishment on an external party, the serpent, then on the weakness of Eve and Adam. Knowing what we now know about human psychology and the nature of evil, we might say that the fall was inevitable, baked into our very humanity, and not anyone's fault. We might say it occurred as a call to greater awareness of our capacity for sin and greater trust in God's mercy.

Christians asked early on why the good man Jesus had to suffer and die. They would develop doctrines of atonement and of a suffering that didn't really hurt. They would blame the Jews. Surely this horrible Passion happened in some orderly manner, and if we are just faithful enough and smart enough, we can avoid its happening again. We forget that Jesus said his followers also would suffer.

In Isaiah 50:4-9a, a part of the third of Isaiah's four servant songs (verses 4-11), the prophet posed another path to understanding. He named the servant as a teacher who would open the ears of the rebellious. They would look upon his suffering and see, first, that he chose to be struck and abused (verse 6); second, that he didn't hide from it (verse 6); third, that his suffering revealed God as a helper and vindicator (verse 7); fourth, that his suffering wasn't a sign that God was disgusted with him, but rather an occasion for God to show love for him (verses 8-9).

What kind of God treasures the one who suffers? Isaiah depicts a God who doesn't cause the suffering, but when it happens steps in to love the victim. In other words, in our pursuit of cause and effect and linear explanations, we are freed to take God out of the lineup. God isn't at fault. God didn't cause my cancer. God is my help in time of trouble, but not the cause of my trouble.

The servant suffers because that's what happens to all people who live—especially to people who live for others and for God. They suffer. Christians recognize Jesus as the suffering servant of Isaiah because he was sharing in the fragility and agony of being human. He wasn't causing that fragility and agony to go away. He was standing in solidarity with us, because that is what God does.

God didn't kill God's Son so that we would never know sin or its consequences. That isn't how life works. We sin, we fail, we soar, we do our best sometimes, and we often fall to a low level, because that is the way people are. God doesn't rescue us from our humanity. God doesn't condemn us, as Isaiah put it. God helps us, enables us to help others, and sets us free from the crippling illusion of control.

How has living for God or others caused you to suffer?

IRONY ABOUNDS
PHILIPPIANS 2:5-11

Ironies were all around when Jesus suffered and died. He was the innocent man executed like a common criminal. He was the faithful Jew rejected by supposedly righteous Jews. Given the chance to defend himself, Jesus remained silent. Instead of condemning those who condemned him, he forgave them. The Passover Lamb opened a path to liberation that few would choose to follow.

In perhaps the greatest irony, the one who alone had reason to claim equality with God refused to do so. He emptied himself before those who were grasping for fullness. He took the form of a slave before those who claimed all power. He humbled himself before the arrogant. He died at their hands willingly rather than save himself.

The capstone of that package of ironies was that it was this Jesus whom God ordained for humankind to follow. At his name we should bow, not the name of the governor who executed him or the emperor whom Pilate represented.

The ironies didn't end on the day of his passion or even on the day of his resurrection. They continue to this day. Christians have claimed equality with God, using concepts like papal infallibility or biblical inerrancy to speak in God's name and with God's authority. Christians have claimed God's authority to pronounce and execute judgment through events like inquisitions and brutal warfare. We have taken lives to defend our claims of truth—claims God never made. We have developed rituals to celebrate our institution, doctrines to declare its absolute authority, and armies to wage war on its behalf. We do all this in the name of one who remained silent before his accusers and helpless before their brutality.

It is tragic beyond measure, and we don't seem to be learning anything from it. From Palm Sunday to Easter Sunday, we will make grand sounds on behalf of one who chose silence. We will display our wealth and excellent taste for one who took the form of a slave. We will gaze proudly upon our vestments and flowers in the name of one who humbled himself. This goes on year after year, for so long now that we think it's normal. Passion Sunday is our time to recognize how abnormal our ways of remembering Jesus are, how far from his core truth when compared with Jesus' own behavior.

The original story itself is too much to bear. I once led a Passion Sunday liturgy in which a man dressed as Judas Iscariot spent the entire service hammering nails into a cross. When we entered carrying palms, he was hammering. When we read the Scripture, he was hammering. When I preached, he was hammering. When we gathered for Communion, he was hammering. He didn't stop until the last person exited the nave.

"Don't ever do that again," a leader told me.

And yet it was exactly what we should have done. We should have taken all ornaments out of the church and kept them out. We should have stopped singing and listened instead to the hammer blows. We should have ceased our normal church ways. But that would have been too much. By now we are heavily invested in worshiping in our own ways, instead of honoring with our humility the humble suffering servant Jesus was.

How do we expect to make any difference in the world as long as we prevent people around us from knowing Jesus as he actually was?

How can you imitate Jesus as the suffering servant?

THE PASSION NARRATIVE
LUKE 22:14–23:56

All four Gospels can be described, in a sense, as Passion narratives with other material added. That is to say, they all devote a disproportionate amount of attention to Jesus' suffering and death; it is the Passion that is primarily important for each Gospel writer. In other words, the writers set out first to tell about the arrest, trial, torture, death, and resurrection of Jesus. Then they add other material to help explain what that Passion means.

That other material, such as Luke's infancy narrative or Matthew's Sermon on the Mount or the raising of Lazarus in John, is sometimes read as biography. That is a mistake. None of the Gospels was written to be a biography. The non-Passion material was carefully selected to support the author's sense of the Passion's meaning and the audience he was trying to reach.

Each evangelist wrote in a unique time and circumstance and for a unique audience. It's very likely that none of them had actually met Jesus. They depended on oral tradition that was passed down over periods ranging from thirty to seventy years. Because each Gospel tells a somewhat different story about Jesus, we need all four Gospels to gain a deep understanding. Though we don't recognize them as authoritative or inspired, we can even learn something from other gospels like the Gospel of Thomas or the Gospel of Mary.

The center of the story, however, remains the events that ended Jesus' life and began the new day that we know as the Christian era: Jesus' arrest, trial, torture, crucifixion, death, burial, and resurrection. Each evangelist tells the Passion story in different terms. We will focus on Luke's narrative.

The Last Supper (22:14-20)
The Christian church would eventually turn the Last Supper into a liturgical ritual, and every detail would be hotly debated and, to some extent, treated as magical incantation. That rite at times became a reward that could be withheld from unworthy people, thus putting the church in the role of discerning worthiness and punishing unworthiness. That conferred great power on the church. But in the process, what Jesus intended was lost.

The event itself served less institutional purposes. It linked the death of Jesus to the Jewish Passover. Jesus was the new Paschal Lamb, the animal obedient Jews sacrificed in order to recall the Exodus and their salvation from slavery in Egypt. This new meal initiated a new Passover and thus a new Exodus, in which God's people would be liberated from the bondage of sin and death.

By sharing the bread and cup with his disciples, Jesus invited them to share in his Passover sacrifice—not as an audience for it, as later came to pass in the church, but as fellow sufferers whose own obedience, perhaps even death, would set people free. Jesus was passing the baton to his friends, not rewarding them for following him faithfully. Jesus was identifying himself with the sacrificial lamb and his disciples with him. They, too, would be called to give their lives for God's people.

The Hebrews understood God as a maker of covenants. God made a covenant with Noah, another with Abraham, another with the whole people of Israel led by Moses, and a fourth with David. These covenants were the foundation of Israel's existence, as well as Israel's call to be a "beacon to the nations," a living covenant with all of humanity.

At the Last Supper, Jesus proclaimed a new covenant by his blood, signified by the bread and the cup (Luke 22:20). By making a new covenant with his disciples, Jesus was linking himself directly to God the maker of covenants, and he was saying that this "new covenant" took God's participation in life to a new level. As Jeremiah said would happen (see Jeremiah 31:31-34), God's covenant became something people took inside themselves. It would no longer be an external sign, but a new inner reality.

Jesus was forming a "new Christ," if you will, a body of faithful men and women who would carry forward his work in the world, in turn creating even more disciples, until creation was restored to oneness with God. What would that "new Christ" do? It would do what Jesus did, namely, heal, teach, serve the least, suffer at the hands of power, die, and rise again, thereby breaking the bond of evil and setting God's people free. Instead of debating what happens to the bread and wine during the liturgy, we should be asking what happens to us. When we partake, are we transformed, as Jesus wanted?

The betrayal foretold (22:21-23)

Early Christians were puzzled. If Jesus had been so manifestly awe-inspiring and authoritative, why did his ministry end in apparent failure? Why did the disciples fall away from him? Why did the people he encountered turn against him?

All four Gospels contend that Jesus was betrayed by one of his own. How exactly that betrayal came about was in dispute, but the Gospels agree that Judas Iscariot, either by perfidy in his heart or on assignment from Jesus, betrayed Jesus' location to the authorities, thus setting the Passion in motion.

Luke said God had "determined" that one of Jesus' own would betray him, so that Jesus would truly be the innocent victim, the Paschal Lamb (Luke 22:22). The betrayer sat at table with Jesus at the Last Supper, an intimacy that made the betrayal all the more horrifying.

The disciples heard Jesus' prediction as a threat to themselves. Which of them would be the betrayer? Suspicion entered their ranks, and verse 23 shows how self-interest became their concern. This one verse, seemingly a throwaway line, foretells the corruption that would undermine their efforts to keep the Jesus movement going, namely, disharmony grounded in suspicion and a self-defeating viewpoint that put self above God.

True discipleship (22:24-30)

As Jesus moved inexorably toward the final confrontation in Jerusalem, tension arose among the disciples.

The disciples responded to his imminent departure by asking the institutional question: Who will be in charge? Who is the greatest disciple of all? Rather than extract every possible learning from Jesus, rather than stand loyally by him, they looked past him and felt the beginnings of competition. This, too, foreshadowed the life of the early church.

Jesus addressed their concern by teaching about the nature of true discipleship. Kings of the Gentiles lord it over their subjects and think of themselves as benefactors, "friends of the people," for doing so (Luke 22:25). True disciples must become servants, not masters, like the youngest and least important (an example being David, the youngest son made king). Serving at table, as Jesus did, is the mark of the disciple, not dining grandly like a potentate (22:27).

Luke then added some unusual material, which no other Gospel contains. When the heavenly banquet occurs, the disciples will dine as the elect and powerful, given the authority to "sit on thrones overseeing the twelve tribes of Israel" (Luke 22:30). These verses seem to contradict what Jesus just said about being servants and not lording it over others. At the very least they raise the tension that would dominate the church's institutional life, namely, whether Christian leaders are vested with power over others. To Christian hierarchs, the answer was a resounding yes. They claimed enormous power. Jesus, however, seemed to want servant-leaders, not power-leaders. If Jesus conveys royal power on his disciples "just as my Father granted royal power to me" (22:29), he wants them to exercise that power through service and humility.

Foretelling Peter's denial (22:31-34)

Peter's denial was apparently an important story for early Christians. All four Gospels include the prediction that Peter would deny Jesus three times before dawn. Since Peter was the first among disciples, this sign of his denial (even he was scared) and his eventual forgiveness (even he had value in the kingdom) reassured believers that the way was open for them, too. Later, Christianity would fall into a cult of the impossibly lofty saint and the expert, which left regular people feeling small. But Peter's denial underscored the need for humility, not smallness.

Peter's bluster came immediately after Jesus' words about servanthood and how followers would share in his suffering. It also has the impact of underscoring just what terrors Jesus had to overcome.

Sayings (22:35-38)

This material is unique to Luke. The meaning isn't entirely clear. Jesus seemed to be underscoring that this was an unusual moment. Being sent generally meant going without any supports and relying on the care of those being visited. But being sent in this Passion moment meant being prepared with purse, bag, and sword. It highlights the hostility that will emerge toward them as Jesus' followers, mirroring the hostility visited upon Jesus himself. The meaning certainly was lost on the disciples. For us, the earlier instructions about relying on God seem pertinent.

Jesus' prayer (22:39-46)

As he prepared for the final confrontation, Jesus crossed the Kidron Valley to the Mount of Olives. Other Gospels specify that he went to a garden there called Gethsemane, though Luke doesn't have that detail. This was his custom, to go off by himself to pray, while his disciples remained nearby, to learn from his example and perhaps also to stand guard. Using language from the Lord's Prayer, Jesus urged them to pray that they not give in to temptation (Luke 22:40; see 11:4). In fact, they fell asleep. When Jesus saw that, he admonished them again to seek being spared, because they clearly weren't ready for a time of trial.

As for the prayer Jesus said, he showed his inner turmoil and a human level of self-doubt not unlike that shown by Peter (Luke 22:42). He knew what lay ahead, and it troubled him. That made his sacrifice all the more remarkable. He actually expressed a desire to avoid it if possible. Jesus wasn't just going through the motions; he actually was going to feel great pain. He accepted it as God's will for him. An angel gave him strength, and Jesus drew on that strength to go even more deeply inside his turmoil, praying so earnestly that he sweated blood (22:43-44).

The contrast between Jesus and his disciples was stark. While they couldn't stay awake, he went into deep turmoil and accepted what lay ahead. This contrast looks important from our modern vantage point, when we are so easily deflected and distracted by the least discomfort. With our internal bickering and our reluctance to do what Jesus did, we seem as shallow as the sleeping disciples. We should be paying attention to this contrast, and asking what it will take for us to imitate Jesus.

Betrayal and arrest (22:47-53)

Starting with the betrayal and arrest, the Gospel's Passion narrative seems to go into slow motion. Like a family's beloved stories, this one is told in granular detail, both to remember that these events actually happened and to savor each element.

A mob approached Jesus and the disciples. Judas was in the lead, apparently to identify Jesus to those who didn't recognize him. Judas had said the one he kissed would be Jesus. But when he tried, Jesus challenged him: "Would you betray the Human One with a kiss?" (Luke 22:48). In the same way, Jesus challenged the religious authorities in the mob. They could have arrested him at any time, he said, and they didn't need weapons to do so. But they came now under cover of night, well armed, and in a remote place because they were cowards filled with the power of darkness (22:52-53). Their time is at night, "when darkness rules."

In contrast to their deceitfulness, Jesus forbade his disciples to defend him by swords. And he healed the slave whom one of his men struck (Luke 22:49-51). This confrontation wouldn't be resolved by weapons, but by his submitting to the darkness in order to take away its power.

I wonder what the history of Western civilization would have been if Christians had continued to heed Jesus' words against armed conflict and his example of submission.

Peter's denial (22:54-62)

Now comes the denial that Jesus foretold. Peter reneged on Jesus in order to save his own skin. That isn't an unusual human dynamic. Its appearance here shows the human side of the Passion. Not only was Jesus in turmoil at what lay ahead, but his disciples were terrified. Following Jesus along the road was one thing; facing an angry mob was something else. This was the other shoe that would fall when they set about carrying his ministry forward. The powerful and religious wouldn't welcome them.

The point of the denial was the final lines: Jesus turned to look Peter in the eye, and once Peter realized what he had done, he was overcome with remorse (Luke 22:61-62). That exchange of looks is one of the saddest moments in Scripture. Jesus saw that his closest ally had failed him, and Peter saw himself as a coward.

Jesus mocked (22:63-65)

The people might not have known what Jesus looked like, but they heard about his powers of discernment and prophecy. They turned those into mockery, just as evil turns all good things into mockery. The incident shows how helpless Jesus was. He was entirely vulnerable to whatever they chose to do.

Jesus before the council (22:66-71)

The religious authorities tried to trap Jesus in blasphemy, which would have made it easier to seek his execution. But Jesus evaded their trap, as he had done on other occasions. If they wanted to be rid of him, they would have to do it themselves. The chief priest and scribes tried to twist Jesus' words into a self-definition as the Son of God. Luke's audience, however, would see that Jesus had not committed blasphemy. Rather, the Jewish authorities were desperate to be rid of him.

Jesus before Pilate (23:1-5)

Now the religious establishment brought Jesus to the Roman governor, Pontius Pilate, who would have the authority to execute Jesus. They fabricated a charge against Jesus that he had tried to stop the Jews from paying Roman taxes (when he had done exactly the opposite) and that he had claimed to be a king (when actually he had avoided that claim).

Pilate questioned Jesus. When Jesus dodged his question, the governor said he could find no basis for an accusation against him. This drew even wilder claims from the religious authorities, namely, that Jesus had stirred up the people, presumably against the government. Jesus had indeed stirred people up, but not to foment rebellion against Rome or against the temple cult. He had stirred their hopes and hunger for God.

Jesus before Herod (23:6-12)

Pilate used a detail of identity to rid himself of this absurd trial and sent Jesus to Herod, the governor of Galilee. Because Jesus was a Galilean, Pilate could argue that he came under Herod's jurisdiction. Herod also questioned Jesus but could find no fault in him. Mainly Herod hoped Jesus would do some magic for him. When Jesus stayed silent, Herod joined in the mockery and contempt and sent Jesus back to Pilate.

Luke offers an interesting detail in verse 12: that their encounter with Jesus enabled Herod and Pilate to become friends. Creatures of the darkness found each other in the course of shaming Jesus.

Jesus before Pilate a second time (23:13-25)

This second appearance before Pilate revealed the anger and fear that Jesus had stirred among the religious leaders and people. Now the entire crowd was crying out, "Crucify him!" They would rather see a criminal named Barabbas released than the one who had come to save them. Pilate demanded to know what evil Jesus had done. They just shouted all the more, "Crucify him!" At this point, Pilate showed his weakness and gave the crowd what they wanted.

These appearances before Pilate and Herod showed how flimsy were the authorities' excuses for wanting Jesus executed. The reality, as shown by the mob, was that everyone was in a fury against Jesus. He had touched them deeply and exposed their hypocrisy.

Jesus on the way to crucifixion (23:26-31)

The procession to Golgotha stands in stark contrast to the scene just days before when Jesus entered Jerusalem to shouts of triumph. One of the great mysteries of the Gospel stories is how the same people who welcomed Jesus as Messiah could now treat him like a criminal. This shift was a measure of how deeply Jesus had disturbed them by acting out the role of Messiah. They had been waiting for the Messiah, but when he came he frightened them.

When Jesus heard women in the crowd weeping for him, he turned suddenly and told them that worse times lay ahead. For if the darkness could do this to him, an innocent man, they should imagine what the power of evil would do to them. The darkness would be so vengeful that everything would turn upside down; even the bearing of children would become an occasion for despair, and barren wombs a cause for happiness.

Jesus on Golgotha (23:32-43)

The contrast between Jesus' demeanor while suffering and that of his tormentors was overwhelming. He was filled with compassion for them and asked God to forgive them. He understood the blindness that motivated them (Luke 22:34). The tormentors, however, would have none of his forgiveness. They cast lots for his clothing. They mocked him and dared him to exercise his power to save himself.

The two criminals hanging with Jesus expressed this contrast perfectly (Luke 22:39-43). One derided Jesus and challenged him to save all three of them. The other saw that Jesus was an innocent man and indeed a king. He asked only to be remembered. Jesus ignored the one deriding him but said the faithful one would be with him in paradise.

We can imagine early Christians taking solace and delight in the memory of these exchanges. They, too, faced mockery and suffering. But God was with them, and so were discerning people like the second criminal. The measure of their faithfulness wouldn't be applause from the crowd, but being filled with forgiveness toward their tormentors.

Death of Jesus (23:44-49)

It was important to early Christians to know that Jesus had actually died on the cross and not merely appeared to suffer. Luke names the moment he died and supernatural events that heralded his death. He recorded Jesus' last cry of agony, a final submission to the will of God, and the moment he took his last breath. Luke also had a witness, a Roman centurion. There could be no doubt that Jesus had died.

Luke also recounted the immediate remorse of the crowd. They knew they had done wrong. The disciples, by contrast, stood and watched—admittedly at a safe distance—so that Jesus did not die alone.

Luke includes the important detail that women were among those who had followed Jesus from Galilee and now witnessed his Passion. Women also would be witnesses to how Jesus was buried and the first to witness the empty tomb. Women were important leaders in the early Christian communities, as these details and Paul's letters make clear. It's true that they did not hold positions as teachers or apostles, but they led and served in other ways. This is consistent with Jesus' ministry, which held a valuable place for women like Mary and Martha.

Burial of Jesus' body (23:50-56)

Not only was there certainty that Jesus had died, but there was also certainty that his body had been carefully secured in a tomb. In other words, his Resurrection was a real event, not some stealing of his body.

The guarantor of actual burial was a member of the Jewish council, Joseph of Arimathea. He asked Pilate for the body, laid it in a stone tomb, and placed a stone over the mouth of the tomb. Women from the entourage verified these preparations. All was done according to Jewish custom. Jesus hadn't ceased being a Jew just because Jewish religious leaders had turned against him.

This finely detailed narrative makes it clear that Jesus did die and rise again; that the people had turned against him but had come to see their error; that Jesus behaved like a true Son of God, while his

THE GIFT OF NEW CREATION

tormentors among the religious establishment behaved like frightened bullies. Above all, this narrative of Jesus' death justifies a faith based on Jesus' resurrection.

****

When I finally reached Morganfield, Kentucky, and found the visitors' center at Camp Breckinridge, I knew I was seeing only a small remnant of a vast reality. Once an enormous training center for Army personnel, as well as housing one of hundreds of prisoner-of-war camps, Breckinridge is now only an echo of that past. Today it is no more than a few barracks being used by a Job Corps facility—and closed to the public—and a visitors' center that once housed a recreation center for non-commissioned officers. I took a slow tour of the museum, admired large murals painted by German POWs, and read documents describing camp life during World War II and the Korean War.

Seeing such a glimpse was fascinating in its own right. I could imagine my newlywed parents dancing at the NCO center, living in married housing, and doing their camp jobs. I could imagine the walks they took into the lovely countryside; the drives they took across the Ohio River on leaves; and the big, all-important drive they took in October 1945 to Wellborn Baptist Memorial Hospital for the birth of their first child.

In seeing these specifics, I sensed but didn't comprehend the enormity of the camp life: young men going through infantry training, large cadres of uniformed men and women supporting them, a large array of civilians, as well as the farmers who gave up their land for the war effort. The scale was almost beyond imagining. How many trains brought in soon-to-be-soldiers, carloads of food, weapons, and uniforms? And similar things were happening all across the country as a reluctant nation mobilized for total warfare.

Luke's passion narrative was like this: a glimpse of something enormous that God was doing. It describes specific actions, like those captured in a slow-motion home movie, and savors each detail, turned over in disciples' hands, like a treasure yielding critical information. And yet the scale was beyond comprehension. God was re-ordering creation, making "all things new," reconciling humankind to God, and seeking to end the enmity among peoples, tribes, and nations. This was more than Israel, more than Jerusalem, more than a single conflict between God's anointed and religious leaders who felt threatened.

I'm not sure we do, or even can, grasp the enormity of God's intentions in those moments. It was, like a nation's total war effort, beyond anything we can see by standing at this intersection or on that hill. But we are steeped in the specifics. We know the story intimately, treasure its details, and tend to imagine the narrative as the full story. It tends to be jarring when we learn that at other intersections and on other hills, other people are having different encounters with God. Much of our warfare arises from the failure of imagination that ensues when we defend our intersection against all others and claim with breathtaking aggressiveness that our narrative is the only narrative.

The question we should all ponder is this: Having glimpsed the more, can we then imagine the more? Or at least leave open the possibility of more?

How can you step back from the specifics and seek something beyond your comprehension?

GROUP STUDY GUIDE

Questions for Discussion

1. Humans have always struggled to understand suffering and God's place within it. How do you make sense of suffering?

2. What does Jesus' identity as the suffering servant tell us about God's response to human suffering?

3. When have you imitated Christ and lived as a servant for others? Did you experience any pain as a result?

4. Review the reflection above on Philippians 2:5-11 and the various ironies that surround the Christian faith. What similar ironies do you see in the world around you or in your own life?

5. How can we live in a way that honors and imitates Jesus' life as a servant, who chose the way of humility and even death rather than exploit his equality with God? What does such a life look like in today's world?

6. What parts of the Passion narrative resonate the most deeply with you? Why?

7. Reading Luke's version of the Passion, what was something you have never noticed before?

8. What is the best way for us to remember and commemorate the gravity of Jesus' suffering and death? How can this become a serious part of our faith not just at Easter, but beyond?

Suggestions for Group Study

Read and Pray the Passion Narrative

Read the Passion narrative in Luke 22:14–23:56 slowly out loud, taking note of its details and pausing at appropriate moments. Divide the story into the sections noted in the reflection above, and have a different group member read each section. Group members may choose not to read a section if they wish. After each section, repeat the following prayer together: "Lord, thank you for your suffering servant."

Continue alternating readers until the Passion narrative is completed, repeating the short prayer at the end of each section. When the reading is finished, allow a few minutes of silence for prayer and contemplation. Then invite group members to share what this experience meant to them.

The Servant of the Lord

The Book of Isaiah includes four "servant songs," short poems that describe an unidentified "Servant of the Lord." The New Testament and Christian tradition has identified the servant as Jesus and have used the servant songs to explain the meaning of Jesus' life, death, and resurrection.

Form four smaller teams, and assign to each team one of the passages as follows:

Group 1: Isaiah 42:1-4
Group 2: Isaiah 49:1-6
Group 3: Isaiah 50:4-11
Group 4: Isaiah 52:13–53:12.

Have each team read their assigned passage and identify characteristics of the Servant. Ask: What is the Servant's role in each passage, and how will the Servant fulfill that role?

Bring the whole group together to discuss their findings. Ask: What similarities and differences exist between the servant songs? How does the description of the Servant change over time, if at all? How do these servant songs help you understand the meaning of Jesus' suffering and death in a new way?

Closing Prayer

O sacred head put to scorn, I cannot just listen to the sound of nails being driven without knowing your agony has to do with me. Your silence before your accusers, your words from the cross, your final breath—those are for me. And I am not worthy. I cannot make myself worthy. I can ask only that you raise me up, and grant me strength to live and die obediently as you have done.

The Gift of New Creation

Scriptures for
Easter Sunday
Isaiah 65:17-25
1 Corinthians 15:19-26
John 20:1-18

Despite everything that has been written about the resurrection of Jesus, it seems unclear to what extent early Christianity was purely an Easter faith.

The Resurrection certainly was central for Paul. Thus it probably was central for the churches he founded, as well. The original disciples and those whom they influenced took heart from Jesus' resurrection. But the faith communities they founded took their lead not only from the Resurrection, but from the way Jesus lived. They, too, became healers, teachers, doers of good, radically tolerant, and inclusive. The Resurrection was the catalyst for the spread of Christianity, but not its sole focus.

That approach faded, however, when Christianity began to function as an institution, or organized movement, rather than an ongoing circle of friends. As an institution in an unwelcoming world, Christianity needed both a hero and a compelling narrative. Easter filled that need. Christians became an Easter people, as opposed to the Jesus people they originally were. They built their institutional life around the events of Holy Week: the Last Supper and Jesus' victory over death. Now it's safe to say that the cross has become our primary symbol, as opposed to the fish, or bread and cup.

The Easter stories of the four Gospels were written down before Easter events became the primary narrative. Note how few verses are devoted to the Resurrection itself, as opposed to the betrayal by Judas, the denial by Peter, the trial, the journey to Golgotha, and what Jesus said from the cross. The first believers were deeply moved by the character of Jesus, likewise by his death on the cross. They were less moved, it seems, by his miraculous rising from the dead.

This might seem strange to our ears, because our faith communities have tended to center around the Resurrection and what it promised about life eternal for those who follow Jesus.

Our opportunity to enter into the ambiguity might happen in Holy Week, when some people are most moved by Maundy Thursday and the narrative of feeding friends and washing their feet. Some find the crucifixion most compelling. In recent years, many Christians have been drawn to the Easter Vigil and its use of flame and silence.

The point isn't to elevate one narrative over another, but rather to highlight how different aspects of the entire narrative touch people differently. The "new thing" that Isaiah saw God doing wasn't just one new thing, but rather a moment of newness when God's will and presence were manifest in fresh ways.

GOD CHANGES LIVES
ISAIAH 65:17-25

From one perspective, what God did on Easter Day was small. No one saw it happen. Only a handful saw its immediate aftermath, and it left them bewildered. Even when people did talk about it, the great majority of humankind were unaware and uninterested.

As time went on, news spread, and a global institution formed to spread that news. We are the beneficiaries of that spread.

How did such a small thing have such a large impact? It wasn't the rising from death, for others had taken that journey. Jesus himself had raised Lazarus (John 11:38-46), and Matthew reports that when Jesus died many holy people rose from the dead (Matthew 27:52). It wasn't the uniqueness of Jesus' teaching, for he said little that was dramatically new. The double command to love God and neighbor appears in the Old Testament (Deuteronomy 6:5; Leviticus 19:18), and other rabbis taught something very much like the Golden Rule. No one remembers his presence as being charismatic, his voice as strong, or his leadership skills as powerful. He spent most of his brief ministry touching a few lives, and even those few abandoned him when their safety was at risk.

His impact certainly wasn't caused by the brilliance of the church that took his name. That church was flawed from its formation. Paul's letters evidence a collection of decidedly imperfect people in the churches around the Mediterranean. Throughout its history the church has withheld leadership from women, demonized nonconformists, tortured, and waged war across the world. Even today, some people take Jesus' name upon themselves and then proceed to do ugly, hateful, brutal, and self-serving things that could hardly be farther from the truth Jesus lived.

I can only conclude that Easter changes lives because God changes lives. God enters into our experience and makes us into something new—not by conveying a convincing story, not by planting a church, but by refashioning creation itself. As Isaiah put it, God creates "a new heaven and a new earth" (Isaiah 65:17). God cuts through old stories and creates anew, as if it were the first day of creation all over again and a new Eden were at hand.

In God's recreation, the tragic city will be "a joy" and its horribly abused people will be "a source of gladness" (Isaiah 65:18). Weeping and cries of distress will vanish. Human life will become a thing to be trusted, and old age a boundless horizon. Isaiah describes an amazing day, in which social inequity will be rectified and life that had seemed futile will be blessed. Even natural enemies will set aside their enmity. The way of the world—a way grounded in hurting and destroying—will disappear from the holy mountain where God's new creation is forming.

This won't happen because God's people "get religion," or repent, or become spiritual warriors, or cleave to truth-filled doctrines, or find perfect worship. It will happen solely because God wants it to happen and makes it happen. The creator isn't asking our permission to refashion creation. God is simply doing it.

That, I believe, is the key to Easter, and it's what should make us profoundly humble as people of faith. As much as we want to control God, rule other people, and make faith a weapon we use to subjugate and judge, the fact is, God is doing what God will do. And we are powerless to cause it to happen or to stop it from happening. We can't reserve it for our kind or deny it to all others.

If God wants to create a new heaven and a new earth, our part is simply to rejoice that God is so gracious and get out of God's way.

This will be bad news for the many who see faith as their excuse for sitting in judgment on those they consider unclean and unworthy. This new heaven and new earth aren't our victory or proof of our righteousness. They are about God.

How are you rejoicing in God's new creation?

A RESURRECTION FAITH
1 CORINTHIANS 15:19-26

In these latter days, people come to faith in multiple ways, and they share their faith with others according to how they began to believe. If they were touched at a retreat, for instance, they believe in the power of such an event to open eyes and hearts to God's existence. To lead someone else to faith, they might well invite them to a retreat. If a small spiritual group or interpersonal relations group was the venue where faith began, they become advocates for such groups.

My own faith came alive in deep conversations with a variety of people, usually in the context of a worshiping community. As I told my story, its connection with God became apparent to me. For that reason, I tend to value small sharing groups in faith communities.

The apostle Paul came to faith through the appearance of the risen Christ to him and the way his eyes were opened as a result. It was central to him that this appearance was in fact Jesus, and that in order for that appearance to happen, Jesus had to have risen from the dead. He became an advocate for a Resurrection-based faith. When anyone questioned whether the events of Easter morning actually happened, Paul responded forcefully. If that Resurrection didn't happen, he said, then we are to be "pitied" and our faith is in vain (1 Corinthians 15:19). He took it as "fact" that "Christ has been raised" (15:20). In that raising to new life, all are "made alive," and by the one new man (Jesus), the death that came from the old man (Adam) is undone (15:22).

Paul didn't see a boundless horizon in which faith would ebb and flow for thousands of years. In his belief, Jesus had appeared and the final denouement had begun. Jesus was raised, the "first crop of the harvest." Then would come "those who belong to Christ" (the first disciples, including those like Paul who came to faith after the events of Jesus life, death and resurrection were over). "And then the end," Paul said, possibly meaning something far in the future, but more likely meaning events happening at that very time, when Jesus has destroyed "every form of rule, every authority and power" and handed a pristine kingdom over to God (1 Corinthians 15:23-24).

"Death is the last enemy to be brought to an end," wrote Paul, and he expected that to happen in his own lifetime (1 Corinthians 15:26). A two-thousand-year time frame—and no end in sight—wouldn't have fit with the urgency Paul felt.

The farther we get from the events of Easter Day, the less likely that the Resurrection itself will be a primary avenue to faith. It's too much an article of history, and to the extent it is experienced today, Resurrection tends to be an argument of the church, buttressed by liturgy, not a felt reality as it was for Paul.

Don't get me wrong: People still can and do come to faith mainly on the basis of the Resurrection. But for more and more believers, faith happens in different ways. For many, in fact, the reading of the Passion and the moment when Jesus gives up the ghost is the holiest, most revealing moment. For others, it is Pentecost. For still others, it is a personal event like a wedding or the birth of a child.

One challenge facing modern Christianity, therefore, is to allow room not only for Paul's Resurrection-centered faith, but for the other ways people walk toward God.

What stands at the center of faith for you?

THE SMALL HUMAN DRAMA
JOHN 20:1-18

All four Gospels tell the Resurrection story as an intimate human drama, as if only the smallest of small stages could convey what God did. Any attempt to capture the grandeur, immensity, and eternal import of Jesus' rising from the dead would inevitably fall short.

The Fourth Gospel's account is the most human and intimate of the four. The emotions it chronicles are emotions we all know from our experience of mortality.

The first emotion was surprise and shock. Mary Magdalene came to the tomb for an unexplained purpose. (In the other Gospels women come to anoint the body of Jesus.) She saw that the huge stone covering the mouth of the tomb had been rolled away. She immediately concluded grave robbers had taken the body of Jesus, perhaps to discredit him, perhaps to add more indignity to his friends (John 20:1-2).

Mary ran to tell the disciples. She gave her message to Simon Peter, already the leader of the Eleven, and to the "other disciple, the one whom Jesus loved," usually identified as John the Beloved Disciple (John 20:2). The nature of their love was never made clear. Neither was Mary's relationship with Jesus. Something intensely personal evidently had passed between Jesus and these two followers.

The disciples react with curiosity, perhaps with a mixture of hope and dread. It's easy to see all of these emotions as Peter and the other disciple raced off to see the empty tomb. John got there first, but Peter was the one to go inside. Both saw the cloth wrappings that had been placed around Jesus' body. This was the first clue that something other than a grave robbing had taken place. John "saw and believed"—though what exactly he believed isn't clear. The author makes a point of saying that neither yet understood that Resurrection had taken place (John 20:8-9).

Mary Magdalene also experiences sadness, or even despair. While Peter and John returned to their homes, Mary remained at the tomb, weeping. She, too, looked inside. Rather than just seeing the cloth wrappings, she saw two angels. They asked why she was weeping. Mary explained her conclusion that someone had stolen the body of her beloved Lord and teacher, and her dismay at not even knowing where his body now lay (John 20:11-13).

Then Jesus appeared and asked her the same question, "Woman, why are you crying?" (John 20:15). This would become the critical question in the days after Resurrection. Should Mary and the disciples be weeping or doubting or otherwise feeling the great loss of their rabbi? Or should they be taking heart, getting up and following Jesus into his new day? The natural human reaction would be sadness. But Jesus was already pointing them to a perspective of faith, joy, and resolve.

THE GIFT OF NEW CREATION

What comes next is among the most poignant, deeply human moments in Scripture. Jesus called her name, and Mary Magdalene knew immediately it was her teacher (John 20:16). Two words: "Mary!" "Rabbouni!" That was the Resurrection event, when Jesus, now risen, became manifest to a friend. Countless words have been written about the events and their meaning. But, in John's eyes, it came down to this: Jesus loved Mary and revealed himself to her, and Mary felt the love in his voice, knew him, and responded.

Their encounter continued with a brief bit of religious language: Jesus asked Mary not to hold onto him, for he was "going up" to the God they shared (John 20:17). The earthly ministry was over. The age of Jesus now gave way to the age of the Spirit and discipleship.

Mary went immediately to the disciples and announced that she had "seen the Lord" (John 20:18). Thus one witness told others, and they, too, became witnesses. This was how the faith spread.

It's intriguing that this account makes it clear that Mary Magdalene, a woman, was the first witness of the empty tomb and the first one to whom the risen Christ revealed himself. She was thus the first evangelist.

I take this to mean that Jesus' inner circle included both men and women, and the women weren't secondary. It's true that the early church made much of the original named disciples being male. But female disciples were named, too. Jesus seems not to have shared his religious culture's dismissal of women as unimportant. They were as close to him as the men were. We'll never know exactly how close Mary Magdalene and Jesus were, but it was close enough that he called her tenderly by name, and she responded in kind.

It's also intriguing that we get a glimpse of how much this parting cost Jesus. His comment to Mary—don't hold on to me—sounds a bit like his sharp rebuke to Peter: "Get behind me, Satan" (Matthew 16:23). Both friends tried to keep him from the stark reality of being Messiah: Peter would have prevented his death, and Mary would have kept him with her. But he pushed on to his death, and he pushed on to his Ascension—at the great cost of leaving his friends behind.

✳✳✳✳✳✳

It was a medium-size congregation populated mainly by young adults. We felt free to try many things. One year we had an all-night Easter Eve vigil, starting with a Prayer Book liturgy and ending with a sunrise celebration of the Eucharist. In between, we improvised.

We had food available, quiet places to pray, books for reading, and corners for sleeping. At around 2:00 A.M., a friend who had become fascinated with the Shroud of Turin offered a video telling the shroud's story and suggesting its mystery; then he led a brief discussion. I recall being awakened for this video and finding it both surreal and mind-stretching. I don't think I came to any conclusions or any ongoing fascination with the shroud. But whether or not this shroud in Turin was indeed the burial cloth covering Jesus' body, one thing did become clear: There had been a body in Jesus' tomb. There had been a burial cloth. And there had been a moment when the body was no longer there. The "how" of that moment seemed less important than the fact itself.

Why argue about a shroud, or indeed about any of the details comprising this Easter narrative? The point remains that the body was there, and then it was gone. Whatever God had intended to do, God had done. That's the overarching point. God did what God wanted to do. Our best response isn't to debate the how, where, and when, but rather to accept God's presence and action.

And then to ponder the why. For that why is the why of our lives. In God's eyes, we are the people who came after Easter. Whatever God intended on that single day, we are the ones to whom, for whom, or by whom God will do it.

Attending Easter service is good, but it's pitifully small compared to God's why. Claiming an Easter faith, maybe being baptized on Easter, knowing the details of the story, and savoring liturgies built around them—all are good, but none of them come close to the fullness of what God intended.

This study, then, ends with the question: Are you ready for that fullness? Are you open to the idea that being a dutiful churchgoing Christian is just a start on the road to fullness that God envisions for you?

How will you embrace the fullness of God's new creation?

GROUP STUDY GUIDE

Questions for Discussion

1. What was the catalyst for your faith? How did you find your way to God?

2. What difference does the resurrection of Jesus make for you? In what way does it stand at the center of your life and faith?

3. How can you reconcile Paul's sense of immediacy for Jesus' expected return with the two thousand years that have passed since that time? What does this say about how we are to live in the present?

4. Have you ever had a quiet encounter with God, such as what John's Resurrection narrative describes? What was that like?

5. In the various Gospel Resurrection stories, the disciples and those who find the empty tomb are both frightened and confused. Why is this? What moved them from these emotions to the joy they would later experience in that moment?

6. Have you ever thought of the resurrection of Jesus as a frightening event? Why or why not? What about this might cause us to respond with fear and trembling rather than, or perhaps in addition to, celebration?

Suggestions for Group Study

Compare the Four Versions of Jesus' Resurrection

Ask for four volunteers, and assign each of them one of the four Resurrection stories found in the Gospels. The stories can be found in Matthew 28:1-10; Mark 16:1-8; Luke 24:1-12; and John 20:1-18. Note that some of the stories continue with further encounters with the resurrected Jesus. For the purposes of this activity, focus primarily on the discovery of the empty tomb. After the volunteers have located their passages, ask them to read their passages out loud to the group.

Identify the similarities and differences among each of the Resurrection stories. Pay attention to things like the characters involved; the moment Jesus appears (if at all); the setting; the mood; the emotions that the characters experienced; and the implied meaning of the Resurrection event. Discuss the following questions:

What does each Gospel writer uphold as the key aspects of the Resurrection and/or the discovery of the empty tomb?

What surprises you about the emotions the characters experience and their reactions to the discovery of the tomb?

How do we as modern readers make sense of these differences between the Resurrection narratives? What meaning can we find within each one, and within all of them together?

Experience a Quiet Easter Moment

The reflection above suggests that the first Easter was a small, quiet moment rather than the grand event as we so often celebrate it today. Allow group members to have space for such a quiet, deep encounter with the resurrected Lord today.

Instruct group members to go off by themselves and find a quiet spot. Suitable spots will vary depending on your setting. Encourage members to spend twenty minutes in silence, simply listening for God's voice and opening themselves to God's presence. At the end of the twenty minutes, gather the group back together and pray the closing prayer below.

As a variation on this activity, you may choose to keep the whole group together to experience a time of shared silence. You may all journey to a single quiet spot together, or you may alter your gathering space to provide a sense of calm and quiet (such as closing the door, dimming the lights, and lighting a candle). Begin and end the time of silence with a brief prayer, thanking God for the hope of the Resurrection and asking for God's presence to be near to you in this time.

Closing Prayer

O God, if I ever muster the courage to walk with Mary to the tomb, help me to see its emptiness and to wonder why. If I ever hear you calling my name, help me to be amazed and passionate. If I ever am asked what I stand for and what my life is about, help me to shout with the angels, "Alleluia! Christ is risen! The Lord is risen indeed! Alleluia!"

Made in the USA
Lexington, KY
02 March 2019